# FACE TO FACE

# FACE
# TO
# FACE

*A Film by*

# Ingmar
# Bergman

Translated from the Swedish by Alan Blair

Marion Boyars · London

A MARION BOYARS BOOK
distributed by
Calder & Boyars Ltd
18 Brewer Street, London WIR 4AS

First published in Great Britain in 1976 by
Marion Boyars Publishers Ltd
18 Brewer Street, London WIR 4AS

Originally published in Sweden as *Ansikte Mot Ansikte*
by P. A. Norstedt & Söner, Stockholm

ISBN 0 7145 2583 9 Cased edition
ISBN 0 7145 2584 7 Paperback edition

The photographs throughout this book were taken by Arne Carlsson.

The actors are: Liv Ullman (Jenny), Erland Josephson (Tomas), Kari Sylwan (Maria), Aino Taube (Grandma), Gunnar Björnstrand (Grandpa), Ulf Johanson (Wankel), Birger Malmström (Man), Göran Stangertz (Boy), Marianne Aminoff (Mother), Jan-Erik Lindqvist (Father), Sven Lindberg (Erik), Helene Friberg (Anna).

Printed and bound in Great Britain
Photo-litho reprint by W & J Mackay Limited, Chatham
from earlier impression

# PREFACE

*Ingmar Bergman wrote the following letter to his cast and crew before they began filming* Face to Face.

Fårö, Sweden
September, 1975

Dear Fellow Workers:

We're now going to make a film which, in a way, is about an attempted suicide. Actually it deals ("as usual" I was about to say!) with Life, Love, and Death. Because nothing in fact is more important. To occupy oneself with. To think of. To worry over. To be happy about. And so on.

If some honest person were to ask me honestly just why I have written this film, I, to be honest, could not give a clearcut answer. I think that for some time now I have been living with an anxiety which has had no tangible cause. It has been like having a toothache, without the conscientious dentist having been able to find anything wrong with the tooth or with the person as a whole. After having given my anxiety various labels, each less convincing than the other, I decided to begin investigating more methodically.

Another person's vicissitudes came to my aid; I found similarities between her experiences and my own, with

v

the difference that her situation was more obvious and
more explicit, and much more painful.

In this way the chief character in our film began to
take shape: a well-adjusted, capable, and disciplined person, a highly qualified professional woman with a career,
comfortably married to a gifted colleague and surrounded by what are called "the good things of life." It
is this admirable character's shockingly quick break-
down and agonizing rebirth that I have tried to describe.
I have also, on the basis of the material at my disposal,
shown the causes of the disaster as well as the possibilities available to this woman in the future.

For my own part I have benefited greatly by this pro-
cess. The torment, formerly diffuse, has acquired name
and address, and so has been deprived of its nimbus and
alarm. If this opus can be of similar use to someone else,
the effort is not in vain.

To recognize a distant or close acquaintance with a
malicious or pitying smile is of course not so bad either
and can give rise to strengthening comparisons, in which
one's own excellence can be measured by someone else's
wretchedness.

Nor in fact is there any harm in simply letting oneself
be entertained for a couple of hours. Good-looking and
talented actors, who in a credible manner portray sad,
dramatic, or amusing situations, are almost always enter-
taining, however painful the complications happen to
be.

On the other hand, ennui or indifference affect the
film's originator in a terrible way, and it is only fair in
that case that he should be put to shame, publicly
mocked, and the victim of thumping financial reprisals.

What more shall I say? Oh yes, as you can see from the
mere bulk of this book, it will be a pretty long film,
several kilometers by the time it's finished. I've tried in

vain to condense it, but each thing has its size and I have learned to be cautious about interfering in my characters' actions and conversations and steering them. During rehearsal we always find points that turn out to be overclear or unnecessary.

The first part of the film is almost pedantically realistic, tangible. The second part is elusive, intangible: the "dreams" are more real than the reality. In this connection let me add a somewhat bizarre comment. I am extremely suspicious of dreams, apparitions, and visions, both in literature and in films and plays. Perhaps it's because mental excesses of this sort smack too much of being "arranged."

So when, despite my reluctance and suspicion, I go to depict a series of dreams, which moreover are not my own, I like to think of these dreams as an extension of reality. This is therefore a series of *real* events which strike the leading character during an important moment of her life. Here something remarkable occurs.

Although Jenny is a psychiatrist she has never taken this extended reality seriously. Despite her wide knowledge she is, to a pretty great extent, mentally illiterate (a common ailment with psychiatrists; one could almost call it an occupational disease). Jenny has always been firmly convinced that a cheese is a cheese, a table is a table, and, *not least*, that a human being is a human being.

This last conviction is one of the things she is forced to modify in rather a painful way when she realizes in a flash that she is a conglomeration of other people and of the whole world. Frankly, I don't know whether she will be able to bear her realization.

In that case there remains only one fairly poor alternative: she reverts to what, for the sake of simplicity and security, is called Jenny Isaksson, a stifling, static combination of mapped-out qualities and patterns of behavior.

If, on the other hand, she accepts her new knowledge, she lets herself be drawn farther and farther in toward the center of her universe, guided by the light of intuition, a voyage of discovery which at the same time opens her up to the other people in an endless design.

There is a consequential alternative: the endlessness becomes unbearable, the mechanism breaks down under the hardships of the voyage, she tires of her increasingly broadened insight and of the ennui that results from such an insight. She tires and puts out the light, in the respectable certainty that if you put out the light it will be dark at any rate—and quiet.

I think it's important to have said all this, since it is significant for our attitude to the film we are going to make, both humanly and artistically.

I mean that the kind of film we are embarking on offers dangerous possibilities of artistic idea-diarrhea. To decide at every moment what is right and true and proper can be rather tricky. And the effort must not be noticeable either. Everything must give an impression of being natural—and yet be possible for us to create with our limited material resources.

So let's set off on a new adventure.

# FACE TO FACE

*The scene is the Psychiatric Clinic of the General Hospital. It is an afternoon in the middle of June.*

MARIA *is* JENNY *'s last patient for the day. She has obviously been crying; she is sitting hunched up, her arms hanging loosely at her sides. Her dark hair falls over her shoulders, thick and tangled. Her beautiful face is blotchy and swollen.*

JENNY *gazes at the one adornment to the bare white room: an abominable oil painting, presumably donated by some artistically inclined patient, which only adds to the dreariness.*

JENNY *(After a long wait)* We've been sitting like this for half an hour. I have to go soon and we won't have a chance to talk until Monday.

MARIA  Oh, come on!

JENNY  I have no idea what you mean.

MARIA  You know perfectly well I've lost a filling.

JENNY  No, I didn't.

MARIA  Yesterday the nurse came and said I had to go to the dentist.

3

JENNY   Well?

MARIA   You arranged it all, didn't you?

JENNY   Honestly, I don't know what you're talking about.

(MARIA *gets up slowly. Her face is very pale and her eyes smolder with hatred. She spits in* JENNY*'s face.* JENNY *remains seated, more astonished than upset)*

JENNY   Sit down, and let's thrash this out.

(*Quick as lightning* MARIA *seizes a thick looseleaf file that is lying on the table and slams it down as hard as she can at* JENNY*'s head.* JENNY *gets her arm up just in time to ward off the blow)*

JENNY   *(Angry)*   Don't be so stupid!

(*The contents of the file scatter all over the floor. She grips* MARIA*'s shoulder and pushes her down into a chair)*

JENNY   *(Angry)*   Quiet down, Maria!

(MARIA *does quiet down and leans back in the chair, looking at* JENNY *with a hurt expression.* JENNY *sits beside her on a yellow wooden chair)*

MARIA   You're always making excuses.

(*But her tone is no longer hostile. She raises her arm and first lays it against her forehead, then crosses both arms over her head like an unhappy child)*

JENNY   You thought I sent you to the dentist so that he'd give you an injection, didn't you? A sedative. Wasn't that it, Maria?

MARIA   I asked the nurse and she said that I might have to have an injection, and when I said I didn't think it was necessary because the root was already filled, she said I'd better be prepared for an injection anyway.

JENNY   You've made that all up. I've promised that you won't be given injections and pills, and I'll keep my word.

MARIA   Do you know what's so incredibly wrong with you? Well, I'll tell you, because I've figured it out: *You're unable to love!* And by love I mean love and not fuck, though I doubt if you're much good at that either. Do you know what you are? *You're almost unreal.* I've tried to like you as you are, because I thought that if I love Jenny uncompromisingly then perhaps she'll become a little more real, I mean less anxious and more sure of herself. Well, people do, don't they, if they know they are loved, even if it's only a dog that loves them. But not a hope! Jenny looks at me with her lovely big blue eyes, the most beautiful eyes in the world, and all I see is her anguish. Have you never loved *anybody*, Jenny? *(She laughs, stretching out her hand and laying it on* JENNY*'s thigh)* What would you say if I raised my hand and stroked your cheek? What would you say if I lowered my hand and began to fondle your breast? What would you say if I . . . if I lowered my hand still more and began to fondle you between your legs?

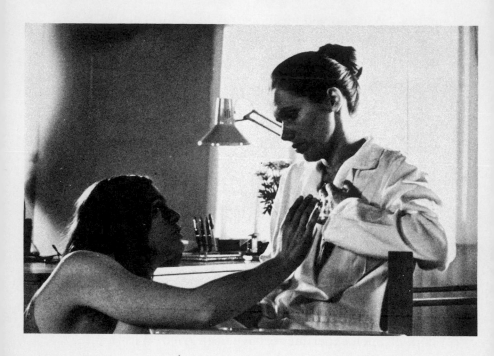

JENNY   You're sweet, really, and very persuasive. But you must remember that a psychiatrist often has to deal with this particular situation. The big problem—and it hasn't been solved yet—is how to avoid involvements between doctor and patient.

MARIA   *(After a short pause)*   Do you like being cruel in the course of duty?

JENNY   Now you're putting it on. You know as well as I do that neither of us would benefit from an affair.

MARIA   Anyhow, in the end you will betray me.

JENNY   What do you mean, betray you? I'm your doctor and I'm trying to make you well. It's *my* responsibility how that's to be done.

MARIA *(Quickly)*   Are you sure? I mean, shouldn't we share the responsibility?

JENNY   That's just idle talk.

MARIA   I mean, shouldn't we share the responsibility— and the risks? Why should I take all the risks and you something vague and harmless called responsibility?

JENNY   It's not practically possible.

MARIA   Why not?

JENNY   Such experiments have been tried. With limited success.

MARIA   With limited success. You're fantastic!

JENNY   What are you doing now?

MARIA *(Quietly)*   So you won't make love to me?

JENNY *(With a smile)*   No, I certainly won't. But if you'd like to continue our inadequate attempts to make you well, I'll gladly do what I can.

MARIA   On your terms?

JENNY   Exactly. On my terms.

MARIA   Look at me for a minute. No, really look. Look me in the eyes, Jenny. What do you see?

JENNY   I see that you're putting on an act.

MARIA   What am I acting?

JENNY   Anguish. Fear. Anguish, I think.

MARIA   And what am I acting now? Look carefully.

JENNY   I don't know.

MARIA   I was imitating you.

*(Laughs)*

JENNY   I couldn't tell that.

MARIA   No, you couldn't. *(Pause)* Poor Jenny!

JENNY   There's nothing poor about me.

MARIA   No, of course not. I'm the one to be sorry for. Isn't it awfully muggy?

JENNY   It looked like there might be a thunder storm this afternoon.

MARIA   Do you never feel helplessly, hopelessly, power-lessly helpless?

JENNY   How do you mean?

MARIA   I mean as a psychiatrist.

JENNY   I don't think so.

MARIA   I'm sure it says on the first page of your first textbook that a psychiatrist must never feel helplessly, hopelessly, powerlessly helpless. And if against all the rules he should feel powerlessly helpless, then he must not admit it. Doesn't it say that on the first page of your basic textbook?

JENNY   Yes, it does actually.

(MARIA *tries to kiss* JENNY *but she pushes her away. Then* MARIA *starts to laugh. Shaking her head and laughing, she bends down to pick up the papers that are scattered over the floor.* JENNY *shoves her aside and picks them up herself. Suddenly* MARIA *leaves the room, shutting the door without a sound.* JENNY *sits down on the yellow chair. She is shaking*)

*That same stormy June evening* JENNY *moves in with her grandparents. They live in a spacious old-fashioned apartment on a quiet street near a park, which borders on the open water and has leafy waterside paths. At the other end is a Victorian church whose tall, slender spire, on early summer mornings, casts its shadow along the entire length of the street.*

*On this particular evening the town is deserted and* JENNY *has no trouble parking her car right outside the ornate entrance of the apartment house. She lifts her suitcase from the back seat and locks the doors.*

*She walks into the lobby with its heavy and now rather shabby elegance: marble staircase, brass banister, thick red carpet, stained-glass windows, paintings on the walls, mosaic on the floor, oddly shaped wall sconces shedding a dreary light over all this splendor.*

*The elevator cage creaks down and stops with a sigh. The grille door is drawn aside and a large woman dressed entirely in black gropes her way out. She is holding a white cane.* JENNY *checks her impulse to help the old lady, as she seems to be quite at home. With her feet now on firm ground she walks with astonishing speed toward the stairs, grasps the banister without hesitation, and begins her descent to the street door.*

*She turns around as though aware that someone is watching her. Her face is strong and very pale. Her right eye socket is staring and empty. Spotting* JENNY, *she gives a faint smile and turns at once to the door, which she opens without difficulty.*

GRANDMA *is a lively, handsome woman with clear eyes and cheeks that are still smooth and rosy. She embraces her granddaughter delightedly.*

GRANDMA    If you knew how pleased I am to see you! Both Grandpa and I have been quite excited all day. Come along and I'll show you. I've put you in Karin's room. You won't be disturbed there and now in the summer there's no noise from the street. Would you like a firmer pillow? I seem to remember that you—

JENNY    No, thank you, Grandma, that's fine.

GRANDMA    Let me see now ... I've cleared out the bureau and one of the closets. I can empty the other one too if you don't have enough room. They're only old summer clothes, I don't know why they're still here, it would be much better to—

JENNY    Grandma dear, one closet and the bureau will be plenty.

GRANDMA  If you need a larger desk we can move in the one from Karl's room. He's not likely to come this summer and perhaps you—

JENNY  I can manage quite well with this desk.

GRANDMA  Promise to tell me if there's anything you need. Grandpa and I have been looking forward *so* much to your coming.

JENNY  So have I.

GRANDMA  Now let's go out and say hello to Grandpa.

JENNY  How is he?

GRANDMA  I think he's better. *(With a little laugh)* You know, he's become so terribly nice.

*(Entering* GRANDPA *and* GRANDMA'*s drawing room is like entering the world that died out with the First World War. Curtains, hangings, carpets, furniture, pictures, wall sconces, and a chandelier. The tall French doors, the ormolu clock, the open fireplace, the mirrors, the small statuettes, the countless photographs of children and grandchildren, friends and relations. The vases of flowers and the potted plants. Everything here lives its quiet, meek life in the soft daylight and the dusk of long evenings.*

*GRANDPA is sitting in a large easy chair. The only sign of his recent illness is that he is very pale; he is immaculately dressed and shaved. Beside the chair is a low table cluttered with books, newspapers, and some old albums, as well as a glass of straight whisky.*

*GRANDPA reaches out with his hand and draws* JENNY *to him. As they embrace, his spectacles slide down crookedly. They are both somewhat moved)*

JENNY   Hello, Grandpa! I've come to stay for two
months. (Erik) sends his love. He's in Chicago at a
conference. I just spoke to him on the phone
and he said he has a lot to tell you when he comes
home. Grandma says you're feeling much better,
and you look it. You'll have a cup of tea too, won't
you?

(GRANDMA *gives him the tea on a little tray, which she places
over the arms of the chair. On a plate are two slices of toast
with jam)*

GRANDMA   And how is little Anna?

JENNY   She went off to riding camp yesterday and has
just fallen in love with a boy three years older than she
is. He tells her all about the world revolution. Things
couldn't be better.

GRANDMA   Is the boy at the camp too?

JENNY   Grandma dear, don't worry. Anna is fourteen
and can take care of herself.

GRANDMA   Do you take sugar?

JENNY   Yes, please. Three lumps. Grandma! Have you
made muffins! Just when I've decided to diet.

GRANDMA   I never heard anything so silly.

JENNY   Anyway, after riding camp Anna is going to stay
with her best friend in Skåne and won't be home until
school starts.

GRANDMA   And when will the new house be ready to move into?

JENNY   I *hope* at the beginning of August. The builders have sworn on the Bible at any rate. Though you never know.

GRANDMA   And you're going to work the whole summer?

JENNY   Yes.

GRANDMA   Won't you have any vacation at all?

JENNY   Oh, Erik and I might go to Taormina in October. We'll see.

GRANDMA   Just what sort of job is it?

JENNY   I'm filling in for the medical supervisor of the Psychiatric Clinic at the General Hospital.

GRANDMA   I hope you're well paid?

JENNY   Yes, thank you, Grandma, I'm very well paid.

GRANDMA   How do you like it?

JENNY   I'm the sort of person who likes it wherever I am. I take after you.

(GRANDMA, *who has finished her tea, has begun darning socks. She glances at her granddaughter over her spectacles*)

GRANDMA   What's the matter?

JENNY   With me? I'm just fine.

GRANDMA   Is something wrong between you and Erik?

JENNY *(Laughing)*   No, certainly not!

GRANDMA   There's something, anyway.

JENNY   I'm just a little out of sorts. I never really recovered from that bout of flu in the spring. So possibly I need vitamins or something.

*(A grunt is heard from* GRANDPA*'s chair.* GRANDMA *gets up at once and goes over to him. Then she calls to* JENNY.
GRANDPA *has opened an old photo album. There are pictures from a summer long ago, when* JENNY *was a little girl and the big house in the archipelago was full of children and grownups)*

GRANDMA   I think that was the summer of forty-eight. Yes, it must be that summer, because Greta is pregnant and Ragnar was born at the beginning of September. What a lot of us there were then! And that wretched boat we had that was always breaking down. How I detested it.

*(*GRANDMA *says this teasingly and* GRANDPA *gives a sardonic smile. Then he points a long lean finger at a snapshot of* JENNY, *eight years old. The little person stands there so incredibly thin and slight, looking delightedly into the camera. She is holding a man by the hand)*

GRANDMA   You were always your father's girl.

JENNY   Oh, there were reasons for that.

GRANDMA  Grandpa loves to pore over those old photographs. He can sit looking at them for hours.

*How about ET?*

(*She strokes his cheek briefly and resumes her darning.* JENNY
*remains standing by the chair, letting* GRANDPA *dip into the
past*)

*It is later that evening and* JENNY *can't fall asleep. Finally she
gets up and pads out to the kitchen. She heats some milk in a pan,
takes liver pâté and gherkins out of the refrigerator, and butters*

*a piece of crispbread. Then she sits down at the big kitchen table,*
*switches on the little portable radio standing on a shelf by the*
*window, and lets herself be soothed by a Mozart sonata. To*
*divert herself further she fishes out an old magazine and spreads*
*it on the table.*

*The window is slightly open to the warm night. It has begun*
*to rain. Now and then thunder rumbles in the distance.*

*The door opens and* GRANDMA *peeps in. She is wearing a dark*
*green full-length dressing gown. Her hair, still tinged with red,*
*has been plaited into a thick braid.*

JENNY  Hello! Would you like a sandwich and some
milk?

GRANDMA  No, I think I'll make myself some coffee.
Nothing puts me to sleep better than a nice strong cup
of coffee at this time of night.

JENNY  Is Grandpa asleep?

GRANDMA  For fifty years I've never been able to figure
out when Grandpa is asleep. He goes to bed, lays his
hands on his chest, and looks like a king lying in state.
It's useless talking to him then. He withdraws into
himself and shuts himself in.

JENNY  I thought he looked awfully tired.

GRANDMA  The paralysis is much better and sometimes
we can actually have a conversation. But you know
how impatient he is. He gets so angry if you don't
understand what he means.

JENNY  How do you cope with being a full-time nurse?

GRANDMA   Oh, he can't boss me around just because he's sick.

JENNY   Don't you ever wish you were a little freer?

GRANDMA   That Grandpa was dead, you mean? Having someone to look after like this, to get cross with or pat on the cheek or just to talk to—it's important.

JENNY   I think so too.

GRANDMA   I'll tell you something. Grandpa never became the famous scientist that everyone expected. He was much too impatient and arrogant. I grew pretty tired of him during those years. In fact I very nearly left home with all the children. He was really impossible.

JENNY   But you never did leave?

GRANDMA   No, I didn't.

JENNY   Did something special happen?

(GRANDMA *helps herself to the last of the coffee and glances at* JENNY. *She gives a short laugh, almost embarrassed.* JENNY, *who for the first time in ages feels warm and relaxed, also begins to laugh. She takes* GRANDMA*'s hand*)

JENNY   Tell me now.

GRANDMA   I went around feeling cross with Grandpa day after day because he kept grumbling about everything, about money and housekeeping and the children's clothes and my appearance and I don't know

what. And I was pretty tired—I had my own teaching
job to do, and we had just moved to Uppsala and everything was in a muddle. Well, one day I was hurrying
along Garden Street, I think I had to go home during
lunch for some reason . . . Oh yes, Linda had the
measles and she was such a mama's girl.

JENNY    And then?

GRANDMA    Well, I happened to look up and there he was
walking along on the other side of the street. I was
coming from the school and he was on his way to
Queen Street, so he had his back to me. Then he
turned the corner.

JENNY    Was there anything special about the way he
looked?

GRANDMA    Grandpa? No, not at all. He walked briskly
along, his back straight and his nose in the air as usual.
Very dapper and with his hat at the proper snobbish
angle. Oh no, he looked just as stuck-up as usual. I
expect you understand this much better than I do,
having taken your doctor's degree in all the little
quirks of the mind. Maybe it has a Latin name.

JENNY    There's nothing about love in our textbooks.

GRANDMA    I see. Hmm . . . Well, I wouldn't call it love
exactly. Rather a kind of understanding. I suddenly
grasped the meaning of all sorts of things: my own life
and Grandpa and his life and the children's future and
the next life and I don't know what.

JENNY    Have you known all that ever since?

GRANDMA   I have to make a terrific effort to remember how I felt then.

JENNY   It was a saint who said, "Love is a state of grace. Those who are in it usually do not themselves know they are among the chosen. Love influences through their actions just as naturally as the rose through its scent or the nightingale through its song." I think it was St. Francis.

GRANDMA   A state of grace? Whose grace?

JENNY   For St. Francis there was no doubt.

GRANDMA *(Respectfully)*   Well, that just goes to show. For me life has been mostly practical considerations.

JENNY   Oh, yes.

GRANDMA   Well, it's bedtime. I'd better close the window, in case of thunder and more rain.

(GRANDMA *gets up quickly and shuts the window. They put out the kitchen light, kiss each other good night, and go their separate ways. The rain is heavier now and a faint rumble echoes over the rooftops)*

JENNY *stretches out on the large, comfortable bed. She picks up a book but finds at once that she is too sleepy. She gives up the attempt and puts out the light. Yawning, she turns over on her stomach and falls asleep immediately.*

*She wakes up feeling completely paralyzed. Opposite her bed, in the changing, shadowless nocturnal light, she can make out a shapeless, gray, billowing mass. Now it takes form, rising, collecting itself. It is a large woman dressed in gray. One eye has been gouged out and the socket gapes black. With excruciating slowness she turns her terrible face toward* JENNY *and gazes at her. Then she speaks. The thin black lips form words which* JENNY *cannot grasp but which seem very urgent, menacing. When* JENNY *doesn't understand, the expression on the woman's face changes to cruel impatience. With great effort she begins to rise from the sofa, looking fixedly at* JENNY, *who (still paralyzed) returns her stare. Now the woman is standing on the floor, her face distorted with fury. She approaches the bed with flowing, unreal movements.*

JENNY *tries to scream but can't make a sound. Just then the apparition vanishes and she wakes up, puts on the light, and sits for a long time bolt upright in bed. It is raining heavily and a gray light is framed against the blind. The time is three thirty in the morning. She gets out of bed and begins to pace up and down the room. Feeling cold, she puts on her bathrobe. She goes out into the drawing room, sits down in* GRANDPA's *chair, and tries to calm herself. "What's wrong with me, I've never been like this, what's the matter with me?"*

*Day is breaking, harsh and gray, outside the big windows. The rain drives against the panes. The ormolu clock gives four quick strokes and is answered by the deep notes of the grandfather clock.*

DR. JENNY ISAKSSON *and* DR. HELMUTH WANKEL *are sitting in* JENNY's *office at the Psychiatric Clinic of the General Hospital, going through the day's schedule. Wankel chain smokes frenziedly, wears thick glasses, and speaks forcefully but with a slight stammer.*

JENNY  Couldn't you try to stop smoking for a while? I'm almost dead from nicotine poisoning.

WANKEL  Jenny, my dear, please forgive me! Let's open the window. Oh, it's open already. I'll empty the ashtray and . . . By the way, how is Maria? I heard that you'd had trouble with her.

*(Ceremoniously, his movements slightly exaggerated, he picks up the ashtray and empties it into the wastebasket)*

JENNY  She has been in my care for two months. When she came in she couldn't make contact in any way and was almost catatonic, with violent attacks of anguish and aggressiveness. Now we can at least talk to each other. *(Pause)* Oh yes! We've stopped treatment of any kind—she is quite unresponsive to . . .

WANKEL    I know. You told me.

JENNY    It's almost incredible. I, at any rate, have never come across that sort of resistance.

WANKEL    You know as well as I do that we can't have people here untreated month after month. We have to do something to get her out.

JENNY    Maria is a gifted person. Sensitive, clever, emotionally well-equipped.

WANKEL    What's the use of all those excellent qualities if her mind is darkened by anguish?

JENNY    All the same, I think I've made a little progress.

WANKEL    You can hand her over to me when you've had enough.
    And realized how hopeless it is to cure psychoses of her kind. So far there are only mechanical solutions.

JENNY    Do you think they deserve to be called solutions?

WANKEL    My dear Jenny. A lunatic quack psychiatrist once wrote that mental illnesses are the worst scourge on earth, and that the next worst is the curing of those illnesses. I'm inclined to agree with him.

JENNY *(Laughing)*    You *are* encouraging.

WANKEL   Twenty years ago I realized the inconceivable brutality of our methods and the complete bankruptcy of psychoanalysis. I don't think we can really cure a single human being. One or two get well despite our efforts.

JENNY   Man as a machine?

WANKEL   Exactly! We change spare parts and eradicate symptoms.

JENNY   Anyway, I'll keep Maria for a little longer. If you don't mind?

WANKEL   You're the boss. For the time being, at least. *(Smiles)* Will you excuse me if I go now? I'm having lunch with the housing minister (an incurably normal neurotic). Besides, I'm dying for a cigarette.

JENNY   Bye-bye.

WANKEL   Bye-bye. And as I said, hand Maria over to me when you're tired of her. Preferably before Erneman returns from his trip to Australia. It has dawned on him that this is a factory which must pay its way and he likes to see the lunatics turn over. That's why he's so well loved by all the politicians and can gallivant all over the world spreading his gospel.

*(He sighs gently, gathers up his papers, and stuffs them into a brief case which seems already about to burst. Then he lights a cigarette and sucks at it frenziedly)*

JENNY   Well, good-bye.

*(Fans herself)*

WANKEL   Oh, by the way. You're coming to my wife's little party, aren't you?

JENNY   As you see, I have on my Sunday best just in case. Are *you* going?

WANKEL   It would hardly be proper, as she's going to unveil a new lover. Young Strömberg.

JENNY   The actor!

WANKEL   The very same.

JENNY   Why, he must be—

WANKEL   He is exactly thirty-six years younger than my wife. It's all rather touching. *(Gravely)* I mean touching. Without any sarcasm.

JENNY   But isn't young Strömberg—

WANKEL   Yes, he is. Elisabeth loves Strömberg's little playmates too. She's like a mother to them all.

JENNY   Then I'll have to go.

WANKEL   You can tell her from me that I have a poor prognosis for young Strömberg and that I love her in spite of everything.

*(He goes off, lighting a new cigarette)*

MRS. WANKEL *opens the door herself. When she sees* JENNY *she bursts out laughing. (Should anyone wish to know what she looks like, she's a small, lively, warm, and friendly woman with short gray hair, a round childish face, and merry brown eyes)*

ELISABETH   Jenny! Well, this is a nice time to show up!

JENNY *(Confused)*   Wasn't it five o'clock?

ELISABETH   No, it was two o'clock, and nearly everyone has gone. But come in. How nice to see you. What a smart outfit. Is it new? And how pretty you are! My God, if only I looked like you! Darling, I *am* pleased to see you. *(Kiss)* Where's your husband? Oh yes, of course, he's in America. How nice.

*(Laughing both from friendliness and from having had a lot to drink, she takes* JENNY *by the arm and leads her into the studio, which is on two floors and full of fashionable furniture and objects. The walls are crowded with her paintings, which express a mild joie de vivre. Over all this the early summer sun. The doors onto the roof terrace are wide open, letting in a breeze from the harbor.*

*One or two guests have lingered and* ELISABETH *hastens to introduce them)*

ELISABETH   This is Mikael. I'm madly in love with him actually, and he's so sweet to me it's just unreal, and this is his best friend and his name's Ludvig. He does *not* like to be called Ludde. The three of us are off to the Bahamas in a few weeks. This is Tomas, you must have heard of him, he's the one who travels around the developing countries teaching the girls how to use contraceptives, it's all frightfully interesting, besides he's the sweetest doctor in the world if you have any trouble with love, you know what I mean. And this is—no, I have no idea, Mikke my poppet, do you know who this is, oh well, let's not disturb him, he's taking a nap, and I should think so too, after the way he abused us all just now, he's *very* committed, you know. These are a couple of charming girls, and *so* clever, who have just opened a boutique around the corner. *(Whispers)* There *is* something about those young girls in their low-cut blouses. Imagine if we were to—fancy if you and I—

*(She bursts out in a snorting giggle and hugs* JENNY *to her as she draws her over to the bar, which extends along the whole end of the lower floor)*

JENNY   And now you're happy?

ELISABETH   I say it only to you, Jenny, because you understand that sort of thing. Naturally we have problems.

JENNY   Oh?

ELISABETH   Cheers, Jenny!

JENNY   Cheers, Elisabeth.

ELISABETH   He's so *complicated*, Mikael. Sometimes I'm almost afraid of him. You know, that Ludvig is a bad lot, really. But you have to take the rough with the smooth. And on the whole I suppose—we—are—what you'd call—happy.

JENNY   How is that, Elisabeth?

ELISABETH   I've come to the conclusion that I'm grateful. *Humbly* grateful, if you know what I mean. Not only for this with Mikael but because I still have myself. I *know* that it's *my* feelings and sensations, since there's no gap between myself and what I experience. Heavens, how badly I'm putting it.

JENNY   I almost envy you.

(ELISABETH *is about to answer when the two awfully clever girls in their décolleté blouses come up to take their leave and she busies herself seeing them to the door.* JENNY *is left alone for a moment. She sits down in a secluded corner and closes her eyes.*
   *Suddenly she feels that someone is watching her. She turns around. Obliquely behind her* DR. TOMAS JACOBI *has ensconced himself in a deep armchair. He smiles encouragingly.* JENNY *returns his smile)*

TOMAS   How are you?

JENNY   Fine, thanks. And how might *you* be?

TOMAS   I'm always well.

JENNY   So what shall we talk about now?

TOMAS   We have an excellent topic.

JENNY   Oh?

TOMAS   You have a patient who happens to be my half-sister.

JENNY   Maria?

TOMAS　Yes.

JENNY　It seems improper somehow to discuss a patient in this setting.

TOMAS　*(Cheerfully)*　We don't have to.

JENNY　Meaning?

TOMAS　We can have dinner together. There's a nice little fish restaurant just around the corner.

JENNY　Well, I *was* going to—

TOMAS　Of course. Some other time then. I'm in town till the middle of August. Good-bye, Jenny.

*(He gets up with a smile and leaves her. She now sees that his left leg is lame; it seems stiff and hard to maneuver. He exchanges a few words with* ELISABETH, *kisses her on the cheek, and limps to the hall, where he looks around for his cane. On an impulse* JENNY *gets up quickly and hurries over to him)*

JENNY   Wait for me down at the restaurant. I'll just make a phone call. If the offer's still open, that is?

*(*TOMAS *looks at her with a smile, then nods in confirmation and opens the front door.* JENNY *goes to look for* ELISABETH, *who is in the kitchen attended by her two boys. She is busy clearing up, neat person that she is)*

JENNY   May I use your phone?

ELISABETH   Why of course, darling. Use the one in the bedroom and you won't be disturbed. I'm afraid it looks like rather a mess, the boys started trying on all my underwear just before the guests arrived. *(Laughs)* They gave me quite a fright—they threatened to appear in drag—in my evening dresses!

*(*JENNY *goes into the bedroom. It is certainly messy. She finds the telephone on the floor, half shoved under the sofa)*

JENNY   Hello, Martin! What luck I caught you. Sorry, but this evening's off. What? Yes, it's a patient. What? Have I met someone who's more fun? Don't be silly now, Martin. Jealousy is most out of place between us. *(Laughs)* Yes, I know you were joking. Bye-bye, darling! *(Puts down the receiver)* Dear God! Dear God in heaven!

*(At that moment* ELISABETH *opens the door a crack and peeps in, smiling delightedly. Then she enters)*

ELISABETH   Are you having dinner with Tomas?

JENNY   Were you listening?

ELISABETH   Darling, you look so frightfully *guilty*, it's *too* exciting!

JENNY   *(Laughing)*   Do I?

ELISABETH   Tomas is crazy about women. But *terribly* mixed up!

JENNY   That sounds nice.

ELISABETH   In the days when I was married to Carl, Tomas was young and ill-mannered and very temperamental. And so sensitive! So sensitive that I . . . well, never mind. Good-bye darling, take care of yourself. I'll call you next week to see how it went.

*(They embrace warmly and kiss each other.*
     ELISABETH *sees* JENNY *to the door.* MIKAEL STRÖMBERG, *the young lover, floats up to his mistress's side. He puts his arms around her and gives her a smacking kiss on her snub nose, saying that he must pop down and buy cigarettes before the store at the corner closes.* ELISABETH *puts her hands on his hips and shakes him gently, with great tenderness, asking if he has money. Yes, he has.*
     JENNY *and* MIKAEL *go quickly downstairs)*

MIKAEL   You're a shrink, aren't you?

JENNY   Yes, why?

MIKAEL   I've got a friend who could use some advice.

JENNY   I'm afraid that will be difficult. I have no private practice.

MIKAEL   Too bad for my friend. I've been watching you. You seem nice.

JENNY   Do I? Thank you!

MIKAEL   Do you have time to talk?

JENNY   Five minutes.

MIKAEL   Let's go into the courtyard. We can sit there.

*(The courtyard is planted with trees and shrubs, and has a little fountain which has already gone to sleep for the evening. The old apartment houses rise around them. There stands a little white bench.* MIKAEL *offers* JENNY *his last cigarette. She declines. He takes it himself and smokes for a while in silence.* JENNY *steals a glance at her watch)*

JENNY   Well?

MIKAEL   I'm worried about something.

JENNY   Does it concern your friend Ludvig?

MIKAEL   No! I've never known anyone less afraid of death than Ludde.

JENNY   So your friend is afraid to die.

MIKAEL   Exactly.

JENNY   And it worries you.

MIKAEL   Do you think someone can commit suicide out of fear of death? It sounds crazy, but do you think it's possible?

JENNY   It's not unusual.

MIKAEL   Anyone who's constantly afraid of dying can't get much pleasure out of living.

JENNY   No.

MIKAEL   It's like a disease.

JENNY   Shouldn't your friend see a doctor?

MIKAEL   Christ, yes. He runs from one clever quack to the next, babbling about his fear of death.

JENNY   Well?

MIKAEL   Oh, they listen ever so kindly and prescribe tranquillizers. *(Looks at her)* Seriously, Jenny. Isn't there any cure for this hellish suffering?

JENNY   So the friend is you.

MIKAEL   Yes, my darling. You're pretty shrewd after all.

*(He smiles with his beautiful mouth and the big blue eyes grow dark with fear)*

JENNY   You can call me on Monday at the hospital. Here, I'll write down the number. You'd better call just after eight in the morning. Then I'll see what I can do.

MIKAEL   But what am I supposed to do in the meantime?

JENNY   Is it that bad?

MIKAEL   Yes. Suddenly time stops, the seconds are endless. It's like sitting in an airplane when the engines fail. Every step I take—every word I say—every moment . . . Funny, isn't it? I'm the luckiest person in the world. It's summer. Elisabeth is the kindest little mother imaginable. I'm extremely talented. Tomas, the old dinosaur—you saw him upstairs—we were friends for a time, he's sort of a humanistic desperado and actually he has also tried to . . . Well, he says that the only way to get rid of your fear of death is to love life and live as if you were never going to die. All very well for him to talk. That's how it is, Jenny! I'm afraid to go to sleep in case I never wake up again. And I know it's inevitable. I, I, I, Mikael Strömberg, will die at any moment, somehow or other. It's no use crying or running and hiding. If I believed in something great it would be different. Sometimes I know just how it smells.

JENNY   Smells?

MIKAEL   The smell of death. The stench of a corpse. I look at my hand, I put it to my nose, and I can smell it, sickly sweet and nauseating.

(*The anguished blue eyes, the handsome actor's face, the well-trained voice*)

JENNY   Call me on Monday.

MIKAEL   Jenny!

JENNY   Yes?

MIKAEL   Are you never afraid of death?

JENNY   No, I don't think so. I'm like most people, I
suppose, who regard death as something that happens
to others but never to yourself.

MIKAEL   Do you have to go now?

JENNY   Yes, I must.

MIKAEL   So long then, Jenny. Thanks for the talk.

JENNY   You'll call me on Monday. For sure.

MIKAEL   For sure.

(*He gives his most enchanting smile and quells the anguish in
his big blue eyes.* JENNY *is suddenly unsure*)

JENNY   You won't do anything foolish?

MIKAEL   Foolish? Oh, I see! No, no, don't worry, darling. At the moment it's one mad whirl. I won't be
alone for a second.

JENNY (*Getting up*)   Weren't you going to buy cigarettes?

MIKAEL   Yes, but I'll sit here for a while and rest. Rest
my ears from that delightful monkey-chatter up there

on the fifth floor. I love it—oh, I love it all right—but sometimes it makes me sick, if you know what I mean.

JENNY  Bye-bye.

MIKAEL  Beware of Tomas!

JENNY  Oh, why?

MIKAEL  He's a real Alice in Wonderland. Though duller, if you get what I mean.

JENNY  No.

MIKAEL  Give him a kiss from me!

JENNY  *(Laughing)*  Give it to him yourself! Bye-bye.

*(They both laugh and* JENNY *leaves the actor to rest after his big scene.*

*Now she is standing in the street. It is narrow and winding, lined by tall old houses. The air is still warm from the sun, despite the gathering dusk. The clock of the neighboring church strikes eight. People stroll past her. She takes a few steps, then stops. She has half a mind to turn and disappear around the corner.*

*But* TOMAS *has already seen her. He has been waiting outside the restaurant, half hidden behind the low awning)*

TOMAS  Shall we go in or are you going to stick to your impulse to run away? You can do as you like. I'll be disappointed, of course, but I won't crack up. They do a delicious fillet of sole.

JENNY  I'm ravenous.

TOMAS  Well then, let's eat, and see what happens. All right?

*(With so many people away for the summer, the little fish restaurant is nearly empty.* TOMAS *and* JENNY, *in good spirits, have dined on the famous sole and a vintage wine. They are having coffee.* TOMAS *is smoking an expensive cheroot.* JENNY *is indulging in a small glass of brandy)*

TOMAS  And what would you like to do now? Shall I take you home or would you care for a little drive out of town? My house is nicely situated but rather dilapidated. We can sit on the veranda in the twilight and listen to music. I can even promise complete silence if you find that more agreeable.

JENNY  You talk like a book.

TOMAS  It's just a way of speaking. I'm rather shy, you see.

JENNY  *(Smiling)  You* shy?

TOMAS  Believe it or not, but I *am* rather shy. I live so much alone, you see. And what about yourself?

JENNY  I'm not given to talking. The reason is that I too am rather shy. Besides, I'm not used to being in this situation.

TOMAS  What situation?

JENNY  Dining with a strange man. I feel rather daring, to be quite honest. What's more, I haven't made up my mind whether to have a bad conscience or not.

TOMAS *(Gaily)*  Some people regard a bad conscience as an extra spice to the enjoyment.

JENNY *(Protecting herself)*  Won't you tell me about Maria?

TOMAS *(Sighing)*  Where shall I start? She was generally considered very gifted. She dabbled in writing and acting and had one or two dramatic love affairs and equally dramatic breakdowns when the young men tired of her. Just between the two of us, I must say I don't blame them.

JENNY  Oh?

TOMAS  Maria's mother died in tragic circumstances— she killed herself. Maria, who was very young at the time, came to live with us. We have the same father, as you may have gathered. Then it got to be absolutely hellish.

JENNY  I see.

TOMAS  Oh, I can't complain. I was mostly away from home, first at college and then abroad, but Maria provoked my parents and my younger brother until they almost lost their minds.

JENNY  What do you mean by provoked?

TOMAS   Love as elephantiasis. Kindness as cruelty, self-sacrifice as selfishness. Concern that becomes an octopus. I don't know. Sometimes I wonder if I'm the one with something wrong and Maria's normal. That bothers me even more, of course.

JENNY   Do you feel sorry for her?

TOMAS   I don't know. As a child I saw a dog being killed. They shot it. Several times. It didn't die. It kept howling and looking at us. Finally someone poured gasoline over it and set it on fire. *(Smiles)* Shall we go?

(TOMAS *lives in an old-fashioned, tumble-down house surrounded by an overgrown, neglected orchard)*

TOMAS   The house is falling down with age and disrepair. Now and then I think about moving to something more modern, but that's as far as it gets. What would you like to drink?

JENNY   Nothing, thanks.

TOMAS   Some coffee, perhaps?

JENNY   No, no. Later maybe.

TOMAS   Do sit down. That's the most comfortable chair. That one's mine. Just ignore it. I'm the only one in the whole world who thinks it's comfortable.

JENNY   Do you play?

*(Indicating the grand piano)*

TOMAS   No, it was my wife who played.

JENNY   Is she dead?

TOMAS   Hmm? Oh. No. We got divorced some years ago.

JENNY   And that was as much of a success as everything else?

TOMAS   The actual divorce was the most successful part.

JENNY   My husband is away for three months.

TOMAS   So you implied at dinner.

JENNY   Actually I miss him very much.

TOMAS   Oh, I'm quite sure you do.

JENNY   All the same I've taken a lover who isn't half as nice. Can you understand that?

TOMAS   Yes, up to a point.

JENNY   To put it bluntly, he's a bore.

TOMAS   Well then, get rid of him.

JENNY   No, he'll do—until the middle of August. Then Erik will be home.

TOMAS   Do you have any other remedy for your anguish? Here—and there.

*(Indicates breast and abdomen)*

JENNY  We're moving into a new house in the fall.

TOMAS  How nice.

*(Confused pause)*

JENNY *(Smiling)*  You're so very polite. Are you bored?

TOMAS  Not at all. I'm just wondering about your breasts. I imagine they're very beautiful.

JENNY  To satisfy your curiosity I can tell you that they *are.* And with that you'll have to be content.

TOMAS *(Sadly)*  You misunderstand me, but never mind.

*(There is a long, awkward silence. They toast each other.* JENNY *goes over to the window and looks at the garden in the twilight)*

TOMAS  Would you care for a cigarette?

JENNY  No, thank you. I don't smoke.

TOMAS  Sensible. Very sensible.

JENNY  Sensible or not, I'm going home.

TOMAS  Jenny! Wait!

JENNY  I'm very tired.

TOMAS  May I drive you?

JENNY  That wasn't the idea. Please call me a taxi.

TOMAS   Will you listen to me? Just for a moment.

JENNY   *(Wearily, with a smile)*   Well, what is it?

TOMAS   Couldn't you and I be friends? No, don't sneer. I'm serious, I mean it. Jenny! Are you listening?

(TOMAS *is still smiling, but his face is tormented.* JENNY *is very angry, tired and angry. She returns his gaze. She is smiling also)*

JENNY   Oh yes! I just want to know how we get from here to your bedroom. I also want to know what fantastic method you have for getting over the absurdity of undressing. Then of course I want to be told what technique you'll use to satisfy me—and yourself. And what you expect *me* to do—just how progressive and creative you will let me be, so that in my sudden passion I don't frighten you.

TOMAS   You're very amusing.

JENNY   A pity, because I'm being serious. Oh yes! Please tell me also how we are to wind it all up when the sex act is over. Is it to be tenderness and silence—a cigarette glowing in the gray morning light—or will it be nervous small talk about the next time as we exchange phone numbers?

TOMAS   You really won't let me drive you home?

JENNY   No, thank you. I *want* to take a taxi. Besides, you've been drinking.

TOMAS    Good-bye, Jenny, my dear. And thanks for a pleasant evening. I hope to see you again sometime.

JENNY    We could go to a movie.

TOMAS    Or a concert. There are some very good concerts in the summer.

JENNY    That would be nice.

TOMAS    I'll be in touch.

JENNY    *I* might call *you* up.

TOMAS    That *would* surprise me.

JENNY    Then perhaps I'll call you for just that reason.

TOMAS    The taxi's here.

(*They go out onto the steps. It is already daylight, but the sun has not yet risen*)

*The sun makes an intricate pattern on the gently ageing wallpaper of the drawing room. The clocks tick; the time is a quarter past three. It is very quiet in the big room, which is so full of strange and unreal things. The birds are singing loudly and defiantly in the park.*

*JENNY has sat down in GRANDPA's chair without taking off her coat. She has simply found herself there, and gone on sitting. She is not sleepy in the least, only tired. Her eyes ache slightly, but she cannot close them. Her hands are clenched on top of the smooth surface of her pocketbook.*

*The door to* GRANDPA's *room is opened without a sound, as
if by a ghost. After a few moments* GRANDPA *shuffles slowly in.
He is in his bathrobe and slippers and his fluffy gray hair makes
a cloud around his old head.*

JENNY *does not make her presence known, and is well hidden
in the big chair.* GRANDPA *stops by the window and stands there
for some time, looking out onto the street. The orange rays of the
sun outline his profile and his skinny neck against the dark wall.*

*Then he rouses himself, as though leaving his sad thoughts
behind. He makes his way to the grandfather clock out in the
dining room and fumbles for the key. Then he begins slowly to
wind it up. At that moment the door of* GRANDMA's *room opens
and she comes padding out.*

GRANDMA *(Crossly)* What are you doing up at this hour?

GRANDPA The clock—

GRANDMA My dear, we wound it properly last night. It's
not good for it to wind it too often.

GRANDPA It keeps stopping.

GRANDMA No, it doesn't. We had a watchmaker here
who overhauled it and said it was one of the best
grandfather clocks he had ever seen.

GRANDPA It loses time.

GRANDMA It keeps the same time as the other clocks,
but if you insist on tampering with it, then it's sure
to stop.

*(He sits down stiffly and cautiously on a dining chair,
his head bent in shamefaced submission.* GRANDMA *sits beside*

*him and waits. After* GRANDPA *has sighed for a while and
vented his anxiety in various ways, she takes his hand gently
in hers)*

GRANDMA   I'm not going to put you in a home. It's all
your imagination, do you hear?

GRANDPA   But we can't afford . . .

GRANDMA   What nonsense. Don't you remember that
the lawyer was here last week and told you that our
finances are very good?

GRANDPA   He's even more senile than I am.

GRANDMA   Oh no, he isn't.

GRANDPA   Isn't he?

GRANDMA   No, he isn't.

GRANDPA   So he's clearheaded, you mean.

GRANDMA   Yes.

GRANDPA   *(Sighing heavily)*   I'm so damned ashamed.

GRANDMA   You have nothing to be ashamed of.

GRANDPA   Not with you. But with all the guests.

GRANDMA   Now you're being silly. Jenny isn't a guest.

GRANDPA   There's so much worry in the house.

GRANDMA  You're anxious just because you've been sick, that's all. It's summer now and in August we'll go down to the country. That will do you good.

GRANDPA  Old age is hell.

(GRANDPA *has begun to weep; he weeps despairingly like a child, at the same time trying to control his outburst, ashamed of his tears.* GRANDMA *sits still, holding his hand between hers)*

GRANDMA  There, there, never mind now. There, there, now, you have me. I'm always with you, you know that. There's nothing to worry about.

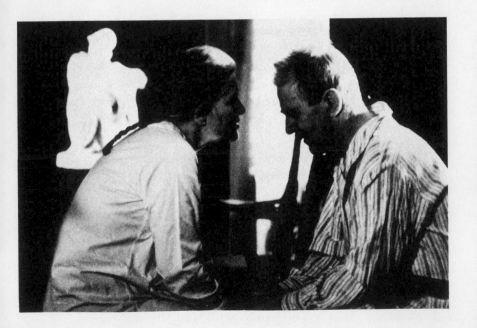

(GRANDPA *keeps crying for some time. Then he stops, tired out, and leans his head against* GRANDMA*'s shoulder. She strokes his head and cheek*)

GRANDPA   Forgive me.

GRANDMA   Come in and lie in my bed, you'll feel easier and get to sleep better.

GRANDPA   I'll just snore and keep you awake.

GRANDMA   I've had quite enough sleep already. Come along now, and I'll make you nice and comfy.

GRANDPA   I get so angry.

GRANDMA   There's nothing for you to be ashamed of. Have you taken a pee?

GRANDPA   I don't need to.

GRANDMA   You'd better go all the same. Otherwise you'll have to get up the minute you're asleep.

GRANDPA   Can't I decide *anything* for myself!

GRANDMA   Well, don't shout so. You'll wake Jenny.

GRANDPA   I'll go and take a pee anyway. And I'll do it to please you. As always.

GRANDMA   Careful how you stand up. Off we go now.

GRANDPA   The grandfather clock keeps losing time.

GRANDMA   I'll call the watchmaker tomorrow.

GRANDPA   There's no need to *rush*. I don't walk as well as I used to.

*(They disappear into* GRANDMA *'s room, murmuring together. After a while there is the sound of the toilet being flushed. Gradually all becomes quiet.*

*The sun rises higher and higher. The pattern on the wall changes and deepens, moving sideways. The birds in the park have fallen silent. It is in fact very quiet.*

JENNY *has dozed off, sitting in the chair. Suddenly she wakes up in alarm. The telephone is ringing. She looks at the clock and sees that it is almost six. When she lifts the receiver all she can hear at first is someone breathing. She says hello, but there is still no answer from the other end. Music can be heard in the background. Suddenly someone giggles faintly. A man's voice says something to her, then the receiver is put down.*

JENNY *stands for a moment or two at a loss, aware of a nasty, creepy feeling. Her eyes are aching with fatigue. Then she makes up her mind.*

*At this hour of the morning the streets are still empty. It is already very warm. The sunlight quivers over the town.* JENNY *drives her little car quickly and determinedly. She reaches the deserted house within twenty minutes. She puts the key in the lock, opens the door, and enters.*

*First she searches the ground floor. It is empty and silent; a few flies are buzzing against the dirty windows. Outside, the summer foliage is dense and protective. She hurries upstairs. She finds* MARIA *on the floor of what used to be the bedroom. She is lying on her side, curled up like a fetus. Her eyes are half open and show no sign of reason. After a quick examination* JENNY *gets up and goes into the next room, where the telephone rests on a chair that has been left behind.*

*She sits down on the chair, puts the phone in her lap, and dials the number of the hospital.*

*It is then that she discovers she is not alone. A man of about fifty is standing in the doorway. Another man can be glimpsed in the background. He is much younger, almost a boy)*

THE MAN   Who are you calling?

JENNY   I must get Maria to the hospital as soon as possible.

THE MAN   What's the hurry?

JENNY   She's unconscious. What have you done to her?

THE MAN   So you're sure we're the ones who gave her a fix?

JENNY   Whoever it was, she must be gotten out of here.

THE MAN   We can help you. You don't need an ambulance.

JENNY   I'd prefer to handle this my own way.

(THE MAN *goes up to her, takes the telephone, and puts down the receiver)*

THE MAN   Don't be scared, I won't hurt you.

JENNY   I have a suggestion. You get out of here at once and I'll take Maria with me. I won't report you for housebreaking, I won't even let on that I've seen you.

(THE MAN *squats in front of her. He smiles.* THE BOY *has come into the room and shut the door behind him*)

THE MAN   Listen to me for a minute.

JENNY   I don't know that I'm interested.

(THE MAN *reaches out and draws his hand across her face in a rather brutal gesture*)

THE MAN   No, you're not interested. But anyway, it's like this, whether you want to know or not. Maria came to our place late last night. During the night she got sick and began calling for you and said we had to take her to you at once, wherever you were. So we looked you up in the phonebook and brought her here. No one opened the door, so the guy over there crawled in through a cellar window. When we found out the house was empty I called up the hospital, and after a hell of a hassle I got the number of where you're living now.

(*Suddenly the younger man pushes* JENNY *down on the floor. She tries to get up but he lies down on top of her. She begins to struggle but the older man holds her firmly.* THE BOY *pulls up her skirt and rips her pants.* THE MAN *begins to laugh, finding* THE BOY *'s frantic efforts amusing. He keeps pressing her arms and shoulders hard against the floor. Suddenly* JENNY *stops resisting and lies still. Above her is* THE BOY *'s red, frenzied face. He reeks of sweat, nicotine, and dirt. He has seized her left breast and now begins to suck at it with a desperate sort of hunger, making abortive attempts time and again to thrust into her.* JENNY *looks at the wild, distorted face pressed against her breast, the thick, mousy hair, the forehead, the smooth cheek, and the*

*childish mouth. She gazes at his face for a long, unreal mo-
ment)*

THE BOY   No, she's too tight.

*(He gets up and zips his fly.* JENNY *remains lying on the floor.
The two men go into the next room. They mumble together for
a few moments. Then the older man comes back, carrying her
pocketbook. He opens it and rummages inside. He finds some
bills which he stuffs in his pocket, then drops the bag on the
floor)*

THE MAN   Some women have to pay for a lay. You didn't
know that, did you? *(He bends over her and gives*

*her a long, hard look)* Now you can call your ambulance.

*(He moves the telephone within reach, then goes into the next room. A door bangs, and after a few moments the kitchen door also is slammed. A car starts behind the house and noses its way on the crunching gravel down toward the road.*

JENNY *reaches for the phone and calls the ambulance. She goes into the next room to* MARIA, *who has not moved and is still lying curled up on her side.*

*Then* JENNY *goes into the bathroom and rinses her face, drying it on a handkerchief which she finds in her bag. She stands for a while leaning forward, her arms propped against the sink. It is very stuffy in there; the sun glitters through the misted panes, where a few flies are buzzing helplessly. She has a splitting headache.*

*When the ambulance has driven off she sits down on the solitary chair beside the telephone. She takes a little red book out of her bag and hunts through it. Then she finds the phone number)*

JENNY Hello. May I speak to Dr. Jacobi? Tell him, please, that it's Dr. Isaksson. Jenny Isaksson. Yes.

*(She is kept waiting. She is kept waiting a long time. She fights a violent agitation as she feels a gray panic surging up from her bowels. It tightens and rages, and she is assaulted by a terrible need to scream. She rocks slightly on the chair, brushes her face with her hand several times, sits on the floor, closes her eyes, opens them, fetches heavy sighs as she breathes.*

*Despite all this emotion she manages to steady her voice when* TOMAS *finally comes to the phone)*

JENNY I thought I ought to call you at once. Maria is in a very bad way. I don't know. Probably an overdose of drugs but I'm not sure. She had run away from the hospital. I found her at my place. Yes, in the house. Couldn't I see you? Then I could tell you more. What? Are we going to a concert this evening? Yes, that'd be fine. You can pick me up at the hospital. Oh no, thanks anyway.

*The concert hall is located in a mansion built at the turn of the century, now used as an art gallery. The rooms are crammed with paintings and sculptures from the period. The lawns and trees of the park can be seen through the big windows, and a calm stretch of water gleams in the twilight of the summer evening.*

*The audience fills not only the concert hall itself but also the adjacent rooms, corridors, and stairs.* JENNY *and* TOMAS *have arrived late and therefore find themselves on the broad mahogany staircase leading to the second floor. They are sitting on a short bench on the landing, their backs to the wall. They are pressed close together, as other latecomers have squeezed into the available space.*

*(The pianist plays Mozart's Fantasia in E Minor.) The twilight mixes with the pale light from the big chandelier softly illuminating the many faces around* JENNY. *She is surprised that so many people are listening restlessly and without concentration; they dart glances here and there, touch their faces, fidget, fiddle with invisible objects, as though still captive in the day's impulses and movements. It is better to look at those who have their eyes shut, who have turned into themselves, who are listening, who are in repose, resting in happy thoughts or none at all. There are two young people absorbed in each other, there is an old man by himself, bent and deformed, but dignified in his listening. There is a middle-aged woman with a great loneliness around her and a calm sadness in her face, there is a dark-skinned boy in thick glasses with his eyes turned to the twilight*

*from the big window, his face full of longing. A little girl has
fallen asleep propped against a youngish woman who is perhaps
her mother. She in turn leans her head against a man's shoulder.
They are wrapped in intimate harmony, content with each
other, themselves, and the constant flow of music. There is an
elderly woman heavily made-up and with blue-tinted hair, obviously an American tourist, sitting stiffly, pressed into a corner, and far from comfortable, but she smiles constantly to
herself and her large gray eyes stray quietly from one person to
the next.*

JENNY *has to close her eyes, she must go into herself. But she
discovers at once that that is not the place to be. Something is
going on there that frightens her and makes her giddy. No, not
there. She can't go there. As long as she keeps still, watching
*TOMAS*'s hand with half-closed eyes, all is well. As long as she
has the self-discipline not to turn inward, all is well. It's a
matter now of minute by minute, hour by hour.*

*She knows instinctively that the longer she can put off what
is going to happen at any moment, the better chance she has of
clinging to the reality that is gradually disintegrating. She
knows that this is the most important thing in the world right
now.*


*Then they are driving along in *TOMAS*'s car. It is still light; the
sky is white and red, and a thin bluish veil-like mist hangs over
the trees and the road and the gleaming water. Before they enter
the house *JENNY* checks him with a movement against the hand
that is opening the front door.*

JENNY  Let's not talk much.

TOMAS  Just as you like.

JENNY   You understand, don't you?

TOMAS   *(Kindly)*   No, not really.

JENNY   It's like this: One has to get through certain hours of life.

*(She regards him appealingly, as though expecting him to understand, but he gives a friendly, questioning smile)*

TOMAS   Well, and what of that?

JENNY   There are certain hours or perhaps only certain minutes.

TOMAS   Is it like that? Now?

JENNY   It may be. At any rate I'm thankful we're together.

*(They enter the hall. JENNY gives a little shiver. Tomas takes her by the shoulders)*

TOMAS   You need a drink, no doubt about that.

*(He pours one out and gives it to her. She stands beside him, watching)*

JENNY   Last time we met we were rather absurd. Don't you think so?

TOMAS   I hardly ever think I'm absurd.

*(JENNY moves about the room, touching various objects. Now and then she stops and looks at him, as though making sure he is still there and hasn't vanished into thin air)*

JENNY    Do you have some good sleeping pills?

TOMAS    Yes, quite good. Do you want one?

JENNY    I'll tell you what I'd like most of all.

TOMAS    We weren't going to talk, you said.

JENNY    Give me the pill, or even two if you think I'll
sleep twice as well.

TOMAS    And then?

JENNY    Then let me sleep here with you in your bed.
Without making love. But you must hold my hand if
necessary. Would you consider something like that?

(TOMAS *goes straight out to the bathroom and returns with
a glass of water and some sleeping pills balanced on the palm
of his hand. He takes her brandy glass*)

TOMAS    If you're going to take such a strong dose you'd
better not drink.

JENNY    No, that's true.

TOMAS    Here are a half a milligram of Valium and two
Mogadon. It's usually a good combination. I take it
myself and it has no aftereffects. If you drink some
strong coffee in the morning you'll pick right up.

JENNY    Yes.

TOMAS    There you are.

JENNY    Thanks.

TOMAS   What time shall I wake you?

JENNY   Just before seven. I have to be at the hospital by eight thirty.

TOMAS   Can't you phone and say you're ill?

JENNY   *(Shaking her head)*   If you force everything to be as usual then it *will* be as usual. Don't you agree? *(Looks at him)* That's how it is with me anyway.

TOMAS   Is that how you cure your patients?

JENNY   No. But they're sick. I'm not.

*(They are lying one on either side of the double bed.* TOMAS *puts out the reading lamp. At first it is quite dark, but after a few moments the dusky light outside shows against the blind and soon* JENNY *can make out the objects in the room. She lies silent for some time with her eyes closed)*

JENNY   Something odd happened to me today. *(She turns on her side with her arm under her cheek and fixes her eyes on the bright rectangle of the window)* When I went to get Maria there were two men in the house. One of them tried to rape me. At first I was frightened, then I thought it was ridiculous, and then . . .

TOMAS   *(Turning his head)*   And then?

JENNY   He was all red in the face. He lay pressing his mouth to my breast and trying to thrust into me.

TOMAS   And?

JENNY  Suddenly I wanted him so desperately to do it.

TOMAS  Do you think that was so strange?

JENNY  No. The strange thing was that I couldn't take
him, much as I wanted to. I was all tight and cramped
and dry.

*(Suddenly she begins to laugh. It bursts out as if she had
long been trying to stifle it, a completely dead laugh. She
shakes with laughter, tries to control it, for a moment it is
checked then breaks out again. TOMAS is bewildered. At first
he smiles to keep her company. When it dawns on him that
she is not laughing at the comic side of the situation nor for
the sheer joy of living but that this is something frightening,*

*he switches on the light and sits up in bed.* JENNY *is lying on her back, with the backs of her hands pressed to her face; her long hair is tousled over the sheet, the pillow has fallen onto the floor, her body is racked with suppressed fits of laughter)*

JENNY  I'm sorry. I don't know . . . I can't help . . . What's the matter with me . . .

TOMAS  Try to sit up.

(JENNY *sits up, her back bent, her shoulders sagging, her arms stiff)*

JENNY  I can't think what . . .

TOMAS  Try to breathe calmly now. Take a deep breath.

(JENNY *tries obediently to do as she's told. But a fresh gale of laughter bursts through the deep breathing. Then the wild laughter changes to retching sobs)*

JENNY  No. No. I don't want to. I don't want to.

(TOMAS *tries to hold her in his arms, but she fights to get free, stares at him in alarm, and shakes her head. The whole time she is racked by convulsive sobs)*

JENNY  I want to go home. Please call a taxi. No, you're not to come with me. I can manage by myself. It will pass.

(*She gets out of bed, shivering as though with fever. Just as suddenly as she burst out crying, she now begins to laugh again)*

TOMAS   Should I call a doctor?

JENNY   What! With all the expertise here already. I'm just tired, there's nothing wrong with me. I'll get home and into bed. There's absolutely nothing wrong with me.

*(With a violent effort she straightens her body, then stands quietly for a moment or two as though musing, listening inward)*

TOMAS   How do you feel now?

JENNY   Better.

TOMAS   Say what you like, but I'm going to drive you home.

*(During the drive they say little. When they pull up outside* JENNY*'s door* TOMAS *is about to get out and help her, but she stops him)*

JENNY   I'm much better now. Thank you. I'm sorry I . . . Forgive me. Forgive me for being so silly. Now I'll snatch a few hours' sleep and tomorrow I'll be fine and then I have two days off. *(She leans forward and kisses his cheek)* Next time we'll talk only about you.

*(She undresses quickly and sets the alarm clock. She is in full control of herself, almost in a good mood. She switches on the little transistor radio by the bed, which plays something soft. Daylight shines outside the window. She snuggles down into bed and sinks into a dreamless sleep. Con-*

*sciousness slips away, is smudged out. She breathes deeply.
She wakes up to find* GRANDMA *sitting on the edge of the
bed with a breakfast tray beside her.* JENNY *stares at her,
bewildered and still dazed with sleep)*

JENNY   What is it?

GRANDMA   You slept all day yesterday and evidently all
last night. I was getting worried.

JENNY   What day is it?

GRANDMA   Saturday. It's nine o'clock. I phoned the hospital and said your tummy was upset.

JENNY   Heavens, I've slept right round the clock.

GRANDMA   I've brought you some breakfast.

JENNY   That's sweet of you, but I don't want anything.

GRANDMA   Have some coffee and a piece of toast. It will
do you good.

JENNY   My head's aching.

GRANDMA   You probably have a temperature.

JENNY   If I stay in bed today and tomorrow it will go
away.

GRANDMA   I'm afraid I can't be at home to look after you.
Grandpa and I have been asked to go and stay with the
Egermans at Högsätra, and we can't refuse them.

Grandpa is looking forward enormously to being in the country for a few days.

JENNY    But Grandma dear, I'll be quite all right by myself.

GRANDMA    Will you? Are you sure?

JENNY    I'll enjoy it.

GRANDMA    Everything you need is in the freezer—there's steak and a chicken casserole. And I've bought milk and bread and—

JENNY *(With an effort)* Grandma dear! Have a nice time at Högsätra and for goodness' sake don't go around feeling guilty because of me. I enjoy looking after myself when I'm not feeling well.

GRANDMA    You promise to call me up if you get worse?

JENNY *(With an effort)* I promise. Cross my heart.

(GRANDMA *kisses her on the cheek, pats her head, and looks at her with sharp, clear eyes)*

GRANDMA    There's nothing else?

JENNY    No.

GRANDMA    Are you sure?

JENNY    Quite sure.

GRANDMA    Shall I ask Aunt Erika to drop in and see how
you are?

JENNY    Anything, but not Aunt Erika.

GRANDMA    All right, then.

(GRANDMA *leaves.*
*After a few minutes* JENNY *has sunk into a coma.*
*She is awakened by a golden light pouring into the room,*
*which is almost dazzling. It is Sunday morning and the*
*church bells echo over the empty streets, calling people to*
*matins. She sits up, feeling light in body and head. The room*
*is shimmering with light and her eyes hurt slightly)*

JENNY    It must be Sunday—morning—obviously—the
church bells—I ought to get up and perhaps eat something, I feel rather peculiar but the anxiety is gone and
that's the main thing. One step at a time, then I'll be
all well by tomorrow. A little food. A walk. A nice
book. Perhaps go to a movie.

(*She gets out of bed, managing better than she had imagined.*
*She goes into the kitchen and puts the kettle on, gets out eggs,*
*cheese, and bread, finds the coffee tin—it all goes much better*
*than she dared to hope.*
*The bells clang, the bright sunlight hovers over curtains,*
*carpets, chandeliers, pictures, and statuettes; the greenery on*
*the other side of the street billows darkly. There is not a soul*
*in sight, not a car, not a living creature. She fishes out a thin*
*blouse, a pair of threadbare slacks, and some comfortable*
*sandals. It is getting rather warm, the edge of her scalp is*
*perspiring, while at the same time her hands and shoulders feel*
*cold. Otherwise she feels very well, even slightly exhilarated.*
*She laughs to herself and stretches)*

JENNY   I'll call Tomas. I don't see why he shouldn't take me to a movie tonight. *(She hurries out to the kitchen and takes the boiled eggs off the stove, makes the coffee, sets the table, phones* TOMAS. *He answers almost at once)* Hello, Tomas, it's Jenny. I just wanted to apologize for being so disagreeable last time. I feel splendid. I thought you might like to ask me to a movie this evening. What's that? Oh, how nice.

(JENNY *looks up. In the mirror she sees the drawing room bathed in light. The tall woman is standing where the sun pours in, gazing at* JENNY *with her one eye. Her right eye socket is a black hole.*

JENNY *puts down the receiver slowly and turns toward the drawing room. The figure between the windows is still there. She goes into her room and sits down on the bed, trying to move calmly and composedly. Then she goes back to the drawing room, which is now empty. She looks around her, goes into* GRANDMA*'s room, which is also empty. There is no hideous figure with an empty eye socket in* GRANDPA*'s room either. Stillness, bright sunlight, her heart pounding, she stands at the kitchen table, her hands on the checked oilcloth. The kitchen clock ticks busily, cheerful radio music comes from an apartment facing the courtyard, two little girls are playing hopscotch down on the black asphalt. The sky is white with light.*

*Back in her room, she sits down on a chair by the window and takes out her little pocket tape recorder from under a pile of books with foreign titles. She is quite calm now. From time to time she takes a deep breath. She starts the recorder)*

JENNY   Dear Erik, my dear one. It's easier to speak like this to a tape recorder than to write a letter. It has always been the way with me that whenever I go to put something in writing, the words escape me. In a

little while I'm going to take fifty Nembutal. Then I'll get into bed and go to sleep. I'm afraid you'll be angry with me for this. As far as I know we have never discussed the possibility that one or the other of us might commit suicide—there has never been any call to. All the same, I realize suddenly that what I'm going to do in a little while has been lurking inside me for several years. Not that I've consciously planned to take my life, don't think that. I'm not so deceitful. It's more that I've been living in an isolation that has got worse and worse—the dividing line between my outer behavior and my inner impoverishment has become more distinct. I remember last Whitsun, for instance.

You and I and Anna went for a ramble in the forest.
You and Anna thoroughly enjoyed yourselves. I made
out it was wonderful too, and said how happy I was,
but it wasn't true. I wasn't taking in anything of all the
beauty surrounding us. My senses reported it, but the
connections were broken. This upset me and I thought
I'd try to cry but the tears wouldn't come.

This is only one example picked at random, but the
more I think back, the more I remember. I stopped
listening to music, as I felt sealed up and apathetic.
Our sex life—I felt nothing, nothing at all. I pretended
I did, so that you wouldn't be anxious or start asking
questions. But I think the worst of all was that I lost
touch with our little girl. A prison grew up all around
me, with no doors or windows. With walls so thick
that not a sound got through, walls that it was useless
to attack, since they were built from materials I sup-
plied myself.

I think you should explain all this to our daughter.
You should explain it very thoroughly, you must be
unflinchingly truthful. We live, and while we live
we're gradually suffocated without knowing what is
happening. At last there's only a puppet left, reacting
more or less to external demands and stimuli. Inside
there is nothing but a great horror.

Erik my dear, I don't feel afraid or sad or lonely.
Please don't feel sorry for me—I'm quite content, almost excited, like when I was little and going on a
trip. It may even be that this is a recovery from a
lifelong illness. I give you my word . . .

(*What* JENNY *was going to promise she can't recall, so after
a moment's thought she switches off the recorder, removes the
cassette, and puts it into an envelope, which she seals. On the
front she writes "To Erik" and lays it on the bedside table.*

*Then she goes quickly into the lavatory and gets the sleeping pills and a glass of water. She makes the bed, pulls the blind down three-quarters of the way, shuts the door, straightens up her things, looks around—it is all very neat. She sits on the edge of the bed, after having laid her bathrobe on the chair at the head.*

*She begins methodically to swallow the sleeping pills, first one by one then several at a time. She is breathless and has to rest for a few moments. She looks at herself in the misty mirror of the big wardrobe: her face is calm, almost smiling, her pupils enlarged, her body hunched and shivery.*

*Now she takes the rest of the pills. Half an hour has passed. She sits for a while with her eyes closed and her palms pressed to her thighs)*

JENNY   I'm not afraid. I don't feel lonely. I'm not even sad. It feels rather nice in fact.

*(Then she lies down and pulls the quilt over herself. She sinks quickly down in a dark swirl of dreams and visions)*

JENNY *is in a hurry, is late, and rushes down a long corridor with high walls extending up to the ceiling, where a wan light filters down through broken panes. The floor is of rough boards and very dirty: scraps from meals, old newspapers, cans, patches of sticky oil, piles of garbage. She's in a great hurry, but at the same time must be careful where she sets her foot, and has to hold up her long, dark, red dress, which wraps her in a rustle of flounces and lace.*

*She sees herself in a large mottled mirror: she is dressed for a banquet but her face is pale, almost sallow, and her eyes are feverish. Her hair is tucked into an embroidered medieval hood, which fits closely around her ears and cheeks. Her forehead shines*

*with sweat. Nevertheless it is cold. She sees that the surfaces of
the room paneling, carvings, floors, are covered with hoarfrost
and dirty white snow that has been carelessly swept out of the
way.*

*She opens a door she seems to remember and finds herself in
a large room that is vaguely familiar: it is* GRANDMA *and*
GRANDPA*'s drawing room. Yet it is very different. Everything
is filthy, dilapidated, decayed; a murky half-light seeps in
through the tattered sacking hanging in front of the windows.*

*In the middle of the room an old man is sitting in a large
battered chair. He is wearing an old-fashioned, ill-fitting tail-
coat and his head keeps shaking. At his knee stands a little girl
in a long red dress; she looks now at him, now at a candle which
flickers in a short holder on a small table to the right of the man
(who grows more and more like* JENNY*'s grandfather). The
candle gutters and is almost burnt out: this obviously frightens
the little girl and her grandfather.*

*A musty, damp cold pervades the room. White patches, as of
snow or frost, can be seen on the floor and walls.*

*As* JENNY*'s eyes grow used to the gloom, she sees that quite a
lot of people are assembled. On the sofas, behind the mirror in
the corner by the tiled stove, half-hidden in doorways, she catches
glimpses of faces and bodies: men in ancient tailcoats, women in
peculiar, faded, ill-fitting ball gowns. Behind one of the richly
carved, half snow-covered lintels she can even make out a gaunt,
ravaged face with two huge eyes shaded by a top hat.*

JENNY *turns around; behind her* HELMUTH WANKEL *is standing. He seems very nervous and worried: he keeps biting at a
nail. He also has a bad cold and a cough.*

JENNY    I'm sorry I'm late, but it's such terrible weather.
Some streets are blocked by snow.

WANKEL    Not at all. The best people are always late.

JENNY   It's chilly here, isn't it.

WANKEL   Many people complain that it's far too warm.

JENNY   Excuse me, but what is the nasty smell?

WANKEL   It's the *accelerating necrosis.* All these people
. . . *(Checking himself)* Exactly.

JENNY   So I've come too late.

WANKEL   Unfortunately. The ball is over. But you
haven't missed anything much. I can't really see why
people persist with masquerades like this.

JENNY   Is it a masquerade?

WANKEL   *(Menacing)*   Didn't you know?

JENNY *(Anxious)*   Yes, of course.

WANKEL   And what are you going to do now?

JENNY   I don't know. *(Anxious)* Do you realize this is a
dream?

WANKEL *(Coughing)*   Are you sure?

JENNY   Yes, this is a dream. The whole of this ridiculous
spectacle is a result of my illness. You mustn't forget
I'm a pretty experienced doctor. It's a dream.

WANKEL   One wakens out of dreams, surely?

JENNY   That's just what I intend to do.

WANKEL  You can try.

JENNY  I wake up when *I* want to.

(*A door opens and out of the darkness behind it steps a large man in a peculiar get-up. He has a long, scarred face, a huge nose, and a big mouth. One of his eyes has been gouged out. On his head he has a checked Napoleon hat. The thickset, almost hunchbacked figure is wrapped in a kind of clown costume. He walks into the room on crooked legs. Everyone greets him with horror-filled respect. He turns toward the grandfather and the little girl, who clings in terror to the old man.*
*The candle flickers, about to go out. It grows very still.*
*The big clown smiles at the girl in the red dress, but his smile seems only to add to her terror. The grandfather makes a feeble gesture as if to ward him off*)

JENNY  (*Whispering*)  What is happening?

WANKEL  That which you can do nothing about.

JENNY  I don't want to see.

WANKEL  You don't have to. In a few moments that light will go out. Nothing will happen as long as the candle is burning.

(*At that instant the light goes out. In an endlessly prolonged second JENNY sees the clown with the gouged-out eye make a gesture toward the little girl, who presses herself in vain against her grandfather.*
*JENNY hears herself call out. She turns away, runs a few steps along the corridor, and stops in front of a small door. WANKEL is still with her*)

WANKEL   I'd advise you not to open that door.

JENNY   You keep trying to scare me.

WANKEL   Well, it's your own fault.

JENNY   If I open that door, I'll wake up.

WANKEL   You can't wake up.

JENNY   I can if I try.

WANKEL   Try.

JENNY   I suddenly remember something. *(Pause)* I bungled my suicide.

WANKEL   Not entirely.

JENNY   What do you mean?

WANKEL   Brain damage due to lack of oxygen. Have you
never heard of that calamity?

*(He sits down on a chair and, taking off his glasses, stares
sadly at* JENNY*)*

JENNY   It can't be so horrible.

WANKEL   Oh yes, it can! An absolute mercilessness that
is also self-inflicted.

JENNY   Will I always live like this?

WANKEL   It seems likely.

JENNY  Will I never wake up?

WANKEL  Don't worry, they'll keep you alive by every means they have. Whether you're awake or unconscious.

JENNY  How long?

WANKEL  Until you die. Properly.

JENNY  And how long before that?

WANKEL  Seconds, minutes, years. How do I know?

JENNY  It mustn't be.

WANKEL  Yes. It must.

JENNY  Then it doesn't matter if I open that door.

WANKEL  *(With a weary, sarcastic smile)*  Logically, your argument is unassailable.

JENNY  By the way, do *you* know what's in there?

WANKEL  No, how should I?

JENNY  Then why do you warn me?

WANKEL  We're thankful for the horrors we're used to. The unknown ones are worse.

JENNY  But it may be something better.

WANKEL  Not here.

JENNY   How can you be so sure?

WANKEL   *(Smiling)*   This isn't only *your* dream, Jenny.
   *We're sharing it.*

JENNY   I'm going to open it, anyway.

WANKEL   By all means. You always have your free will.

JENNY   You're leaving?

WANKEL   *(Smiles)*   I don't want to get into a worse mess
   than I'm in already. So if you'll excuse me. *(Suddenly he
   turns around and walks up to her. His face is distorted, his
   pale eyes glare at her malignantly, his breath has an evil
   smell. He shakes his finger at her)* I've been pretty patient
   with you, my dear Jenny. I've answered your foolish
   questions, I've shown you around, I've been kind and
   obliging. But have you *for one moment* been interested
   in how I am? Have you said *a single word* to show that
   you were pleased to see me? Have you *in any way*
   thanked me for my kind warnings? By the way, your
   face is yellow, which is a bad sign. Now I'll go out of
   *your* dream and into my own. Good-bye.

(JENNY *opens the door and steps into* GRANDMA *and*
GRANDPA*'s apartment. It looks the same as usual except for
the light, which is gray and shadowless (like the light on a
rainy day in autumn). She calls* GRANDMA, *enormously re-
lieved; her eyes fill with tears of joy. She calls again, going
from room to room.*
   *Finally she sinks down at the shiny black dining table, her
sallow complexion and dark red dress reflected faintly in the
table top as though in deep stagnant water)*

JENNY   If only I could wake up.

*(She looks around her; everything is familiar but remote and shadowy. She turns her head toward the drawing room opening up beyond the French doors. It is a little lighter in there.*
*In the middle of the room, clearly outlined and tangible in the fluid light, stands the big one-eyed woman, looking at her)*

THE WOMAN   You're cold.

JENNY   Yes.

THE WOMAN   You can have my cardigan.

JENNY   Thank you.

*(THE WOMAN goes up to her and wraps her in a large dark cardigan, which covers the red dress and her bare shoulders. JENNY draws it around her. THE WOMAN sits down on a chair near her)*

THE WOMAN   So *now* you're not afraid.

JENNY   I don't think so.

*(THE WOMAN reaches out her arm and draws JENNY to her in a motherly gesture. JENNY makes no resistance, her head sinks onto the old woman's breast.*
*The long dark cardigan covers her completely. At the same moment someone takes her roughly by the arms and shakes her, calling her name. An agonizing, wavering light that gets brighter and brighter bores through her closed eyelids)*

JENNY   Leave me alone. I don't want to. I don't want to. Can't you leave me in peace. I don't want to.

*(Now she can see a window; the sunlight strikes her face
and burns her eyes. A familiar seeming face appears. It is*
TOMAS.

*She is wet with sweat and can smell a sour stench, the
hospital nightshirt is damp and stained, she can see her bare
feet somewhere far away.*

JENNY *(Trying to smile)*   I think my legs have come off.
Can't someone get them from the corner over there
and fasten them on?

TOMAS   Hello.

JENNY   What are you doing here?

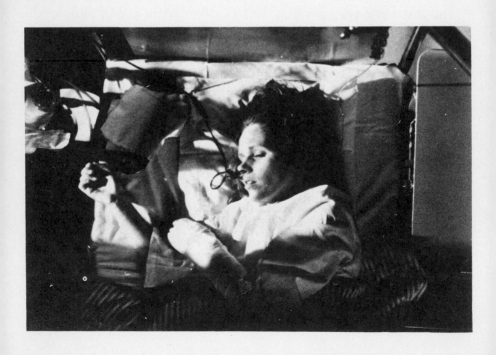

TOMAS   We were going to a movie together. Remember?

JENNY   *(Shaking her head)*   No.

TOMAS   Suddenly you were silent and put the receiver down. I didn't know what to think, though it did seem odd.

JENNY   Oh. *(Wearily)* Oh, I see.

TOMAS   So I kept phoning off and on, but there was no answer. I thought you might have been attacked by a burglar or something—I just didn't know what to think. It was very unpleasant. Are you thirsty? Wouldn't you like something to drink?

JENNY   Yes, please.

TOMAS   Take this. I'll help you. Wait a moment, you can't do it by yourself. Careful now.

JENNY   *(Drinks)*   Thank you. *(Dully)* I am very grateful.

TOMAS   Finally I was so worried that I went and rang your doorbell. When no one answered I got the janitor to open the door.

JENNY   God, what a bore. I'm so sleepy.

*(She succumbs to the temptation, unable to go on any longer. The deadly tedium washes over her. "Oh Christ," she mutters hoarsely and vanishes from the world of the living, leaving TOMAS on the sunlit shore. She returns to the land where the light is like thin ashes and the air is musty, raw, and chill.)*

*She is again in* GRANDMA *and* GRANDPA *'s apartment, again wearing the red dress. She goes from room to room calling her parents in a clear, anxious voice)*

JENNY Mama! Where are you? Daddy! I'm home now. Why are you hiding? If it's a game it's not a nice one. Come out now and don't frighten me like that . . .

*(A middle-aged man in a gray overcoat comes toward her, followed by a somewhat younger woman. They appear suddenly, unexpectedly, and seem intent on running into her and knocking her down.*

*The man is tall but stooped. He has clear blue eyes and thin gray hair; his expression is tense. The woman with him is very beautiful, with regular features and large dark eyes. She also has an anxiously questioning expression.*

*They stop just short of* JENNY *and look back, as if in search of someone or as if they had lost their way)*

JENNY Mama, it's me. Daddy, it's *me!* Don't you recognize me?

*(*JENNY *calls to them, but their anxiety is far too great, they don't hear her whisper. She knows it is very urgent and that she must say the right words)*

JENNY I'm so very fond of you both, you were always so good to me. It was so odd when you suddenly just disappeared. I saw you when you were dead, lying in the funeral parlor. I didn't know you. Mama dear, why are you so anxious? There's nothing to worry about, I'm not nine years old any more. I'm grown up and have taken sleeping pills, it doesn't seem to have come off, they're hard at work on me at the hospital.

You couldn't help being so anxious about everything. Dear little Mama, everything had to be exactly
right and proper and so drearily neat and tidy. And
Daddy who was so affectionate and liked to be
hugged and who was so sad and nervous. We used to
hurt each other without meaning to. Just think, all
our lives, all the days and all the words and little
things. We had nice times too, didn't we? I was a
child, I didn't know what it was all about. *(Furious)*
No, you . . . you just slammed the door and there we
were with the guilt. Always a bad conscience, always
to blame! *(Weeping)* Go away and never come back.
I'm going to forget you so completely that I'll never

have to see your anxious eyes again and never have to
hear your timid voices.

*(Her parents are ashamed and humiliated. They begin whis-
pering furtively to each other and at last reach some kind of
agreement. Her mother buttons her coat and tightens the belt
around her slender waist; her father puts on his hat, which he
has been holding all this time in his left hand; under his right
arm he carries a brief case)*

JENNY *(Wearily and in despair)*   It's always the same! First
I say I love you, then I say I hate you, and then you
turn into two scared children, ashamed of yourselves.
Then I feel sorry for you and love you again. I can't
go on any longer.

*(She strikes at them at the same time as she tries to embrace
and kiss them. They defend themselves lamely and with unreal
gestures. Their clothes tear with a brittle, rasping sound.*
JENNY *tries to hold on to them though they are now retreating
hastily into the darkening twilight.*
    *Finally she trips over her red dress and falls)*

TOMAS   Jenny!

*(She opens her eyes and looks around. It is evening. The ceiling
light is on and the night lamp, with its indirect glow, is also
burning)*

JENNY   What a horrid smell in here, and I'm so nasty and
dirty. Can't you ask them to let me have a wash?

TOMAS   Your husband is here.

JENNY *(Plaintively)*   Not now!

*(But it's too late. The door opens with a faint sigh and a nurse appears but goes out again at once, making room for* ERIK, JENNY*'s husband.*

TOMAS *withdraws tactfully and husband and wife are alone. They look at each other in embarrassment.* ERIK*'s eyes are slightly bloodshot—whether from fatigue after the long plane trip or from sorrow is hard to say. But he is carefully dressed in a lightweight, fashionable summer suit and his hair is well groomed. His weak mouth trembles a little and his face is very pale. He is holding the cassette with* JENNY*'s letter)*

ERIK *(Smiling)* Well, you do have a knack for springing surprises.

JENNY  Yes, don't I.

ERIK  I've come straight from the airport.

JENNY  Poor Erik. You must be awfully tired.

ERIK  No, not in the least.

JENNY  Won't you sit down?

ERIK  Oh yes. Yes, of course.

*(When he has sat down, coming quite close to her, their shyness is, if possible, even more of a barrier)*

JENNY  I smell nasty. I'm so sorry.

ERIK  No, no, my dear, it doesn't matter.

JENNY  Can't you come back tomorrow? By then we'll both have recovered a little.

ERIK   Yes, of course. Though tomorrow I must fly back. It's hopeless! I'm to be the chairman of—

JENNY   Poor you!

ERIK   Oh, I'm all right.

JENNY   The trouble I cause.

ERIK   It would have been awful if you . . . I'd never have . . . In all my life I've never been so . . .

JENNY   Forgive me!

ERIK   Why did you do it?

JENNY  Forgive me. Forgive me.

*(The same tone of voice. The wide dark eyes, the hair, matted with perspiration, straggling over the white brow, the lips sore —a child trapped in the bitter anguish of death. It is too much for* ERIK. *He lowers his eyes and looks at his white hand with the Doctor's ring and the well-tended nails)*

ERIK  *(Quietly)*  I realize I'm largely to blame for this. Though I don't know how. I've tried to think it out—

JENNY  Another time, Erik?

ERIK  Do you think you can rest now?

JENNY  Yes, I think so. Please don't worry. there's no need.

ERIK  That Tomas seems to be a decent fellow.

JENNY  Yes.

ERIK  Have you known each other long?

JENNY  No.

ERIK  Apparently he's a doctor but not here at the hospital. A gynecologist, isn't he?

JENNY  Yes.

ERIK  What do you want me to say to Grandma? She's bound to ask.

JENNY  Tell her the truth.

ERIK  And to Anna?

JENNY  I'll have to talk to her myself. You can just call her up and ask how she's getting along at the camp.

ERIK  Yes, I will.

(*The silence between them grows into a solid transparent wall. They are both pretty worn out with emotion and grief*)

JENNY  Bye-bye, my dear. We'll keep in touch! Eh?

ERIK  Bye for now!

(*And he is gone.*

JENNY *turns her head to the side and closes her eyes. She suddenly finds herself in a low, arched room. Outside the windows it is winter and snow lies thick. The room is lighted by big globes hanging from the ceiling. They give out a dirty yellow half-light which pitilessly exposes the peeling plaster on the walls, the filthy floor, and the stained, colorless cloth on the conference table. A naked woman is sitting in a gynecological chair, covered with a soiled sheet. She is dead, and several doctors in white coats have gathered around her, consulting in whispers.*

*At one end of the table* JENNY *is sitting in her red dress, but with a doctor's coat thrown over her bare shoulders. She now sees that the dead woman in the gynecological chair is* MARIA.

*The doctors sit down at the table. They look through their papers, light cigarettes, drink mineral water, whisper among themselves.* DR. WANKEL *looks at* JENNY *with an interested expression and nods to her encouragingly*)

JENNY  She said she loved me. I admit I didn't understand the significance of that statement. Besides, she
herself did her best to confuse the issue. Please listen!
I have a right to defend myself before the matter is
remitted.

*(The men stare at her in sudden surprise, as though her re-
proach were most uncalled for)*

JENNY *(Vehemently)* I don't see the point of all this.
If I have broken any of the rules, scientific or ethi-
cal, that we have pledged ourselves to respect, then
charge me.

*(No one moves or reacts. No glances or secret understandings.*
WANKEL *props his head in his hand and doodles on a pad. The
glasses of the man next to him catch the light.*
    JENNY *gets upset. She starts to her feet, the chair top-
ples over, the white coat spreads out over the red dress. She
stands for a moment with clenched fists, looking down at
the table)*

JENNY  That soft body, those soft arms, those large soft
breasts. And then that mouth, which was always so
soft and moist and half open. I felt a physical disgust
which I tried to overcome, and when she touched me
I had to fight to control myself, to stop myself from
striking her. *(She is silent, then bends down, picks up the
chair, and sits down)* I'm sure there *is* something called
love. I even think I've met people who love or have
loved. *(She shuts her eyes and slowly puts her hands to her
face. After a few moments of tense silence she lowers them and
speaks harshly)* I've tried to live like everyone else. And
I've failed. Do you think I don't see that myself? *(Cries
out)* I have no words to say what I mean. It's hopeless.

*(Pause)* This is too hard, I'm not equal to it. *(Pause)*
Once only in my life have I *understood* another human
being. For one short moment. Understood a human
being! Do you see . . .

*(The faces turned toward her face. The eyes, the mouths, the
hands. The naked white body gleaming there behind the men's
polite smiles, the closed dead face. Outside the arched windows,
the gray dusk and the snow. All this)*

WANKEL    Have you anything more to say?

JENNY    No.

WANKEL    Then the hearing is over.

JENNY    What happens next?

WANKEL    The case will be passed on to the Committee
on Medical Ethics.

JENNY    And then?

WANKEL    Then? Nothing.

JENNY    Nothing?

WANKEL    No, of course not. That's the most usual.

JENNY    Nothing?

WANKEL    What did you expect?

JENNY    A punishment.

WANKEL   You do presume. Even if we despise each other behind our backs, we must stick together outwardly. You know that as well as I do.

JENNY   Nothing . . . Nothing . . . Nothing . . .

*(When JENNY wakes up from her dream it is night. She sees someone sitting in the visitor's chair and puts on the bedside light to see who it is—perhaps it's a ghost. It is TOMAS. He is wearing an old sweater and has a blanket wrapped around his legs and his feet up on the other chair. Beside him he has a thermos of coffee and some cheese and sausage sandwiches. When JENNY switches on the light he blinks rather sleepily)*

JENNY   What time is it?

TOMAS   I'll have a look. One thirty.

JENNY   What day is it?

TOMAS   Tuesday. It'll be light soon. Tuesday, June twelfth.

JENNY   Oh.

*(Slowly, slowly it dawns on JENNY that it's odd after all that TOMAS should be in her sickroom at one thirty in the early hours of Tuesday, June twelfth)*

TOMAS   How do you feel?

JENNY   I don't know. *(Pause)* Tomas!

TOMAS   Yes?

JENNY   Why are you sitting here keeping watch?

TOMAS   I have my reasons.

JENNY   Oh?

TOMAS   Anyway, I'm your doctor.

JENNY   I didn't know that.

TOMAS   No. But now you do.

*(Both become lost in their own thoughts.* JENNY *is sinking back into her other state, which awaits her just behind the wall. She makes an effort to stop herself)*

JENNY   Do you have coffee in that thermos?

TOMAS   Yes.

JENNY   Do you think I could have some?

TOMAS   No, I think you'd feel pretty sick if you started gulping down a lot of strong coffee. But you can have fruit juice.

JENNY   No thanks.

TOMAS   It's good for you to drink something.

*(He helps her to drink, turns the pillow, goes back to his chair. Silence)*

JENNY   How can you do your work if you sit here day and night?

TOMAS   I'm on vacation.

JENNY   Oh. Couldn't you find a nicer way of spending
it than watching over a mixed-up suicide?

TOMAS   No.

JENNY   Tell me about yourself.

TOMAS   When I was nine I learned to belch. My older brother taught me. One day at dinner I thought
it was a good opportunity to demonstrate my newly

acquired skill to the assembled family. I watched for
my chance between the meat balls and the apple
pie.

JENNY *(Interested)*  Well?

TOMAS  It was not a success. From sheer stage fright I
happened to fart at the same moment I belched. Moreover, the fart was much louder than the belch, which
I rather bungled technically.

JENNY *(Smiling)*  Poor Tomas!

TOMAS  I made a stir but was a failure. I was sent away
from the table and not allowed any apple pie and cus-
tard. My upbringing was very strict, not to say dog-
matic.

JENNY  Tell me more. I like to hear.

TOMAS  I don't know that there's much to tell. My life
has been pretty uneventful. And the little I *have* experienced, I've tried to forget.

JENNY  Anything will do. Perhaps you've just read
something or met someone interesting or been to a
movie or on a trip.

TOMAS  Frankly, it's over a year since anything happened to me.

JENNY  And what happened then?

TOMAS  Someone walked out on me.

JENNY   Oh yes, of course. You're divorced.

TOMAS   No, it had nothing to do with a wife.

JENNY   Oh?

TOMAS   It was a friend who walked out.

JENNY   Oh!

TOMAS   I was very fond of him. *(Pause)* No, that's not true. I loved him. We lived together for five years. You met him at that ridiculous party given by Wankel's wife. I take it you know who I mean.

JENNY   The actor?

TOMAS   Yes. Nowadays we are "just friends."

JENNY   Why did it break up?

TOMAS   In our cruel market, my dear Jenny, disloyalty is total and competition ruthless. Mrs. Wankel offered better terms: she accepted his new friend and offered to support them both. As you know, she has resources.

JENNY   Wasn't he fond of you at all?

TOMAS   Oh yes, I think so. But he's good-looking and unintelligent and pretty spoiled, and I suppose he thought: anything for a change. My emotions and my jealousy were too much for him. (TOMAS *pours himself some coffee out of the thermos, selects two lumps of sugar with great care, and keeps stirring on and on. He is smiling the whole time)* Would you like to sleep?

*(She turns her head to the wall.* TOMAS *puts out the bedside
light. It is broad daylight out in the hospital park and the
birds are singing. They are making an awful noise.*

JENNY *is standing in her office at the General Hospital,
wearing her red dress. There is a crowd of people there.* JENNY
*taps her pen on the desk to make herself heard. The murmuring
stops at once and everyone's eyes are turned expectantly, anxiously, toward her face. She asks in a faint voice who is the
day's first patient, and a man in the crowd puts up a timid
hand. She pushes her way over to him and asks how he is. He
doesn't answer, but puts his hand to his face and begins to pull
at the skin, which comes off. He has been wearing a mask—
very skillfully made—but under the mask his face is disfi-
gured by bleeding sores and festering ulcers. He looks implor-
ingly at* JENNY, *who can hardly hide her disgust. When he
realizes that his sores nauseate her, he meekly takes a large
handkerchief out of his pocket and drapes it in front of his
face)*

JENNY   You may come back in a month. Ask the nurse
for an appointment. Don't forget to take your medi-
cine.

*(*JENNY *turns immediately to the next patient, a woman with
heavy breasts and rounded shoulders; her eyes are dilated with
horror and her cheeks are abnormally taut. A strip of paper
is sticking out of her mouth.* JENNY *takes hold of the end of
the strip and pulls cautiously; something is written on the
paper.* JENNY *pulls more and more of it out of the woman's
mouth)*

JENNY *(Reading)*   Help me! They've made an incision in
my head and cut away my anguish, but when they
sewed my head up again they left the daily dread behind.

*(Suddenly* JENNY *is standing face to face with* GRANDPA. *He looks at her with a hurt expression, then whispers something. She can't hear what he is saying and has to bend closer)*

GRANDPA   I'm afraid of dying.

JENNY   So am I.

GRANDPA   What can I do?

JENNY   Count to ten. If you're still alive when you get to ten, then start again.

GRANDPA   And after that?

JENNY   Just keep on. You just have to count.

GRANDPA   You think it will help?

JENNY   You have to put something important between yourself and death all the time. Otherwise you'll never stand it.

GRANDPA   One two three four five six—*(Breaks off)* I'm still afraid.

JENNY   *(Whispering)*   I must see to the other patients. We're rushed off our feet with Christmas coming on. I don't know what gets into people.

GRANDPA   Yes, I quite understand. Forgive me.

*(*JENNY *turns away. Then she sees her daughter* ANNA *standing over by the wall, dressed in a soiled gray shirt, weeping quietly, her shoulders hunched. At last* JENNY *reaches her and*

*stretches out her arms to warm, protect, and embrace her, but* ANNA *avoids her.* TOMAS *looks at her gravely. She grasps at his hand, which is gloved)*

JENNY   If only for *once* I had the right words. Just for once.

TOMAS   Exactly, Jenny. They're sitting there in the dark, your patients, longing for *the right word*. But it must be *their* word, *their* feeling, not your word and your feeling.

JENNY   I know that loneliness—people's loneliness—that they are brave in their loneliness. Like children in the dark who are determined not to call out lest they grow even more afraid if no one should come. They weep quietly and restrainedly in their loneliness. *(Pause)* A human head is so fragile. To hold someone's head between your hands and to feel that frailty between your hands . . . and inside it all the loneliness and capability and joy and boredom and intelligence and the will to live and . . . *(Pause)* An old person's hand . . . the day has been long and trying but evening comes, the hand that opens. *(Pause)* I can't go on, no.

TOMAS   Once upon a time there was a mighty prince who was tormented by a raging desire for affection. He went out and caught his subjects in big hunting nets and then took them on strings of pack mules to his palace. There he had them tortured, and when they groaned with pain he tried to comfort them with tokens of affection and gifts. What's the matter?

JENNY   I can't take any more.

*(She turns her head and sees the white wall of the hospital room. She is lying in her bed and it is broad daylight outside the window)*

JENNY   What day is it?

TOMAS   It is still Tuesday.

JENNY   And what's the time?

TOMAS   You've slept for two minutes.

JENNY   *(Weeping)* Why are children frightened and killed? How can we pretend it doesn't happen?

TOMAS   What do you mean?

JENNY   That children die. That children are ill-treated. That children starve to death. There's no living with all that. What is it we do to each other? How can I pretend it isn't happening?

TOMAS   I think you're paying for that indifference with an utterly abstract anguish.

JENNY   What's going to happen?

TOMAS   I don't know. When my friend left me, I got into my car and drove it into a deep ravine. I sat there trapped for several hours with water up to my nose. Then I was fished out of the wreck with a crushed foot.

JENNY   That was no answer.

TOMAS    You complain that man is a wolf to man. Objectively, you can't do anything about it. Pity is only coquetry anyway, and mostly ends in a neurotic fiasco. Or political hysteria. It's a matter of taste which you choose. (TOMAS *stops speaking and looks out of the window. In the bright daylight he looks pale and wretched, his eyes are tired and bloodshot and he is unshaven*) Has it never struck you that you are surrounded by overgrown children? They don't starve physically, but mentally. They die. Not that they're shot, but they are slowly and methodically harassed to death in a society which on the whole is just as cruel as in the Middle Ages. On all sides grown-up children and little children being tormented and suffering and dying. Unfortunately there's nothing you can do about it.

(*He has taken off his glasses and keeps blinking.* JENNY *watches him out of the corner of her eye*)

TOMAS    That's how it is.

JENNY    Are your eyes hurting?

TOMAS    Once when I was young and drunk I took a swim in one of the canals in Venice. I should have known better. I caught a chronic virus infection of the cornea. Sometimes it smarts and then I blink.

JENNY    In any case, I don't know what to do.

TOMAS    A million years ago a few spinal marrow cells ran amok in a baboon's head and started dividing like cancers. And all of a sudden there it was!

JENNY    Who, what?

TOMAS   The human brain. A crazy gadget without any counterpart in the rest of zoology. There it was, like a big, damp woolen cap hung up on the simple needs and instincts of the old brain. There it was, sending out messages left and right and every which way. A computer-operated army headquarters with hundreds of thousands of programmed generals, who are supposed to guide a small native tribe through the perils of life and the jungle. The results had to be staggering. And they are.

JENNY   Come and sit here. On the edge of the bed.

TOMAS   Well, here I am. What do you want?

JENNY   Nothing in particular. It's just nice.

TOMAS   *(After a long pause)*   I do see that life has its moments of splendor. With a certain objectivity I admit that it is even extraordinarily beautiful. And generous. Intellectually I can grasp that it offers all sorts of things. I'm only sorry to say that I personally think it's a pile of shit.

*(He stops talking and looks at the wall. Then he looks at* JENNY *with his blinking, red-rimmed, rather dilated eyes.* JENNY *meets his gaze, deciding to look into his right eye, which appears more hopeful than the left.*
   *Then she notices that he is crying. Noiselessly, without his face moving, the tears are flowing one by one, very hesitantly, down his cheeks. He takes out a neat handkerchief and blows his nose and dries his eyes)*

JENNY   *(Astonished)*   Are you crying, Tomas?

TOMAS   No, no for Christ's sake. It's just that eye inflam-
mation. Excuse me if I go to the men's room for a
moment.

JENNY   Tomas!

TOMAS   No, no, don't be silly now. It's stinging like hell.
I'll go out and have a cigarette and get some more
coffee. (*With an apologetic gesture he moves toward the door*)
I'll be right back.

(*In a moment he has managed to withdraw from the room.
Outside the window the morning is overcast. It is raining
tentatively.* JENNY *falls asleep almost at once.
She sees herself lying in a white coffin. It has been set up*

*in* GRANDMA's *drawing room. The windows and walls are covered with sheets, the furniture also is covered over. Bunches of white flowers are everywhere. In all this whiteness there is a group of people dressed in black. The dead woman is dressed in red; in a very wide gown, so voluminous that it swells out over the edge of the coffin in an almost obscene way. On her feet she is wearing red stockings and shoes, her arms are bare and pressed to her sides, the palms turned outward. Her head lies flat, the hair, loose and flowing, is adorned with white flowers. Her eyes are wide open and she follows the proceedings with horrified amazement.*

*JENNY sees now that a* CLERGYMAN *has stepped forward to the coffin. He is wearing an ample cassock and a large silver cross on a chain. He bends over* JENNY *in the coffin. Terrified, she meets his eyes)*

CLERGYMAN   It's possible that she was alive a while ago, but now I can guarantee she's dead. Let us therefore proceed to the ceremony.

*(Everyone approaches the coffin, looking self-important.* JENNY *goes up to* TOMAS, *who is standing in a corner)*

JENNY   This is nothing to grieve over.

TOMAS   It's not for this that I'm crying.

*(The* CLERGYMAN *has brought forth a small box of sand from under his wide cassock. He takes a few fistfuls and tosses them into the coffin)*

CLERGYMAN   Bring the lid, she stinks already. I think they've botched the embalming, as usual.

*(Everyone turns toward a corner, where* JENNY *'s parents are struggling with the lid, which seems too heavy for them. They stagger as they approach with it.*

JENNY *in the coffin makes a panic-stricken movement as though to sit up, but falls back with a faint cry of protest. The lid is lowered. Fussy hands are poked in to stuff the swelling red dress down inside the edges of the coffin. Nevertheless, when the lid is at last in place, a lot of material is still sticking out. There are worried whispers. The* CLERGYMAN *goes over to* GRANDMA *'s work table by the window. Out of a drawer he takes a large pair of scissors, which he hands to one of the mourners, who immediately sets about cutting away the protruding cloth.*

*A faint knocking is heard from inside the coffin but no one takes any notice. They begin to screw down the lid. The* CLERGYMAN *and some of the mourners sing something that is supposed to be a hymn. Suddenly the coffin begins to burn.* JENNY *has crept up and set fire to it! We catch a momentary glimpse of the red dress, a pair of frantically waving arms, a gaping mouth. Then everything is one huge flame.* JENNY *wakes up.*

TOMAS *comes back, bringing a fresh thermos of coffee. He sits down, trying to stifle a wide yawn but not succeeding very well. He smiles apologetically)*

JENNY *(After a long pause)*  As a child I was afraid of death. It seemed to be all around me. My poodle was run over, that was almost worse than anything. Mama and Daddy were killed in a car crash. I told you that, didn't I? *(Pause)* Then a cousin died of polio. I was fourteen then. We had sat under the dining table kissing on the Saturday, the next Friday he was dead. Grandma made me go to the funeral. I begged and pleaded to be let off, but Grandma wouldn't relent. He lay in an open coffin and there were lots of people and his mother kept crying and he looked so funny. Grandma told me to go up to him and look at him and "bid farewell," as she put it. I imagined he was breathing and that his eyelids were twitching. I said so to Grandma. She said it was a common optical illusion and that I should control myself. When they screwed down the lid I knew for sure that Johan would wake up in there in the dark, way under the earth. When we got home after the funeral I told Grandma I hated her. She boxed my ears, hard, and told me not to be hysterical. She was sorry afterwards and apologized. But I never forgave her.

TOMAS You've always been regarded as a miracle of sanity, haven't you.

JENNY I've followed the principle that now I'll make up my mind to feel like this and I feel like this. I decided I'd never be afraid of death and the dead. I decided to ignore the fact that people died every day, every moment. Death didn't exist any more except as a vague idea, and that was that. *(Pause)* Before I got married I lived for some time with a crazy artist. Once when he was angry with me he said, You know, your frigidity is so complete that it's interesting. I was angry too and said, It's only with you that I'm frigid. With other men I get an orgasm. Then he said, It's only in boxing that you can have a technical knockout. *(Pause)* One evening at a party not long ago someone read aloud a poem about love and death and how love and death merge. And include each other.

TOMAS Well?

JENNY   I remember being pretty sarcastic about that poem. Stupid of me. Don't you think?

TOMAS   Yes, perhaps.

JENNY   We act the play. We learn our lines. We know what people want us to say. We lie. In the end it's not even deliberate.

Self-discipline. *(Pause)* Bewilderment. Pride. Humiliation. Self-confidence, the lack of it. Wisdom that is stupidity and the other way around. Arrogance and vulnerability. Easily hurt, *that's* it, terribly easily hurt. Touchy and bad-tempered but inhibited, everywhere inhibited, reticent, paralyzed. Capable. And conscientious. You can rely on Jenny. Just as if she were something real! An airplane engine or a rowboat. Daddy was very kind, and he drank. He liked to be cuddled, we got on well together, he and I. Then Mama would say as she went past, That's enough of that soppiness. And Grandma would go past and say, Your father may be a dear but he's a lazybones, and Mama agreed with Grandma. They backed each other up in despising Daddy and in the end I sided with them. It was as simple as that. And suddenly I was embarrassed by Daddy's hugs and kisses—Grandma thought he was silly and lazy and I was anxious to please her. Then I got a child of my own. Anna had a funny cry, it wasn't like other babies', she didn't cry with rage or because she was hungry and wet. It was more like real sobbing. It was heart-rending and sometimes I wanted to hit her for crying like that and sometimes I was beside myself with tenderness. But all the time with myself in the way. A most peculiar selfish fear: I would not let myself go. And then the joy went out of everything. *(Long pause)* I remember the first time I heard Mama

cry. I was in the nursery and I heard Grandma and
Mama talking and Grandma had a curt, funny tone.
Then Mama screamed. I have no idea what it was
about. I felt terribly afraid, mostly because Grandma's
voice sounded so nasty. I rushed into the living room.
Mama was sitting in a low chair by the window, crying. Grandma was standing in the middle of the room.
When I came in she turned her face and looked at me.
And it was Grandma's face and yet *not* Grandma's
face. *She looked like a mad dog that was about to bite!* I was
even more afraid and rushed into the nursery and
prayed to God that Grandma would get her real face
back and that Mama would stop crying. It's horrible
with faces that change so that you don't recognize
them. Sometimes it sticks in my throat. Sometimes I
think it's disgusting.

TOMAS   What is?

JENNY   The world's going to the dogs and I doctor my
mental ailments. It's disgraceful.

TOMAS   Your logic is hardly dazzling.

JENNY   Oh?

TOMAS   First you try to take your life because of terror,
confinement, and isolation. Then you despise our
efforts to break out of the same confinement, terror,
and isolation.

JENNY   While the world comes to an end?

TOMAS   The world begins and ends with yourself.
That's all there is to it.

JENNY *(Bursting out)* I can't talk about that!

TOMAS You must try.

JENNY I can't, I won't!

TOMAS There's no avoiding it. You must try.

JENNY Leave me alone. Let me be. My head's aching. Can't you give me a shot or something? *(Bangs her head against the wall)* It's more than I can bear. I can't go on.

TOMAS You must. *Nothing is more important!*

JENNY Let me be. You're hurting me. *(Weeping)* Leave me in peace. Let me go, for Christ's sake! You have nothing to do with me. Go away.

TOMAS Jenny, *please.* Jenny, it's important for me too. You can't just slink away.

JENNY I feel so sick.

TOMAS Lie down. Breathe deeply.

JENNY I can't live with this.

TOMAS Slow, deep breaths.

JENNY You can't wear that dress today. It's your Sunday best. You'll never manage that, my dear. Let me help you. Using lipstick, are you? Most unseemly while you're living in our home. Eat up what you have on your plate. You're late again. Will you never learn to be punctual? You're lazy and spoiled. If you go on

like this Grandpa and I will send you to boarding
school, you'll soon learn to mend your ways there, my
girl.

In this house, Jenny, live decent people, people who
have tried to live in cleanliness and truth. You'll have
to behave properly if you intend to go on living here
with Grandpa and me. You should be grateful. If only
for *once* you could show a little gratitude. *(Screams
heart-rendingly)* Don't hit me like that. You're not to hit
my face. I can't stand it. *(A different voice)* I'll teach you
to behave. What's all this nonsense? Stop crying. I
don't believe in those tears.

*(Shouts)* I'll do as I like. You're not going to order me
around. You're a goddamn stupid bitch. I hate you and
I could kill you. *(Whispering)* You'd better decide after
all. Yes, I know you love me. I think you mean well.
I know that I must do as you say. Why, *(complainingly)*
*why* must I always have a *bad conscience? (With hatred)*
I will beg your forgiveness. Forgive me. I apologize. I
know I've done wrong. I always do wrong. I will be
Grandma's good little girl. I'm Grandma's little pet.
We can talk about everything, you and I. With you it's
always nice and calm and safe. *(Turns pale, her eyes go
inward)* I can see all the furniture, all the pictures, I
can see the plate of porridge and the reflection from
the window in the shiny glazing. Mama smelled so
nice and she had small round hands with flat fingertips
and her hands were always warm. *(Whispering)* If you
lock me in the closet I'll die. *(Still fainter)* I'll be good
if only you don't lock me in the closet. Please, please
Grandma, forgive me for everything, but I can't live
if I have to be locked in the closet. *(Lame gestures with
her hands. Pause. Then in a clear voice)* Can you imagine
shutting up a child who's afraid of the dark in a closet?
Isn't it astonishing?

TOMAS  Yes, it's astonishing.

JENNY  Do you think I'm crippled for the rest of my life? Do you think we're a vast army of emotionally crippled wretches wandering about calling to each other with words which we don't understand and which only make us even more afraid?

TOMAS  *(Mumbling)*  I don't know.

(JENNY *bends her head and sits for a long time silent and sad.* TOMAS *leans forward hesitantly, puts out his left hand, and rather shyly begins to stroke her head)*

TOMAS  There's an incantation for us who don't believe.

JENNY  What do you mean?

TOMAS  Now and then I say it over silently to myself.

JENNY  Can't you tell me what it is?

TOMAS  I wish that someone or something would affect me *so that I can become real.* I repeat over and over: Let me become real one day.

JENNY  What do you mean by real?

TOMAS  To hear a human voice and be sure that it comes from someone who is made just like I am. To touch a pair of lips and in the same thousandth of a second know that this is a pair of lips. Not to have to live through the hideous moment needed for my experience to check that I've really felt a pair of lips. Reality

would be to know that <u>a joy is a joy and above all that
a pain has to be a pain.</u>

*(He is silent)*

JENNY   Please go on.

TOMAS   Reality is perhaps not at all what I imagine.
Perhaps it doesn't exist, in fact. Perhaps it only exists
as a longing.

*(The door is thrown open and the floor nurse, VERONICA,
stares—with controlled astonishment, of course—at the two
figures over by the window)*

VERONICA   Sorry to disturb you.

TOMAS   You here in the middle of the night, Nurse?

VERONICA *(Cheerfully)*   The middle of the night?

TOMAS   My watch says only five past four.

VERONICA   Well, I don't know, but outside it's five past
ten.

JENNY   But it *is* Tuesday, isn't it?

VERONICA   Oh yes. I just wanted to tell you that your
daughter is sitting out there and would like to see you.

JENNY   Oh!

*(JENNY is seized with panic for a moment and looks around
as if for a means of escape. TOMAS has stood up and is folding*

*his blanket. He turns to her and is about to say something when* JENNY *anticipates him)*

JENNY   I'd like to talk to her. But not in here. Perhaps we could sit in the visitors' room?

VERONICA   By all means. The old lady who has appropriated it is out walking in the park.

JENNY   I must fix myself up.

TOMAS   Of course, my dear Jenny. I'll go.

VERONICA   Dr. Isaksson, what about a breakfast tray in the visitors' room? Wouldn't you like a cup of coffee? And perhaps your daughter would too.

JENNY   *(From the bathroom)*   Yes, please.

TOMAS   I think we can let Mrs. Isaksson go home today. That is, if she wants to.

VERONICA   Shouldn't I ask Dr Wankel?

TOMAS   I don't think that's necessary.

*(*JENNY *pokes her head out from behind the curtain. She has just washed her face and is holding a towel)*

JENNY   Will I be seeing you?

TOMAS   That would be nice, but it may be some time.

JENNY   Some time, how do you mean?

TOMAS   I'm off to Jamaica tomorrow.

JENNY   You didn't tell me.

TOMAS   I suppose I forgot.

JENNY   So you mean I'll have to manage on my own?

TOMAS   *I'm* the one who'll have to manage on his own.

JENNY   Supposing I come with you to Jamaica?

TOMAS   No thanks.

JENNY   What are you going to do there?

TOMAS   I've heard that one can lead such a wonderful life of vice in Jamaica.

JENNY   But you'll come back?

TOMAS   I won't promise.

JENNY   Bye-bye, Tomas.

TOMAS   Bye-bye. Take care of yourself and those who are fond of you.

*(He goes out quickly.* JENNY *sits on the edge of the bed, feeling faint from getting up so fast and affected by the sudden farewell. Then, pulling herself together, she completes her morning toilet, puts on a hospital gown and a pair of bath slippers, and shuffles out into the corridor in search of her daughter.*

ANNA *is standing with her back to the door, looking out the window. She is tall and lean. She has long red hair, big gray eyes, and a broad forehead, but otherwise soft features, a childish mouth and chin, astonished eyebrows. When she hears her mother's steps she turns around)*

ANNA  Hello, Mama.

JENNY  Hello.

ANNA *(Rapidly)*  Daddy phoned and said you were sick. Since he came rushing home like that all the way from America I thought it was something serious and I'd better come and see you, though Daddy said I shouldn't.

JENNY  Heavens above.

ANNA  You know how Daddy always exaggerates.

JENNY  Did he tell you why I was here?

ANNA  He said you'd been taken ill suddenly and they'd brought you to the hospital in an ambulance.

JENNY  He didn't tell you the reason?

ANNA  No, he didn't.

*(ANNA looks at her mother reproachfully. JENNY sits down in a rather shabby chair. Just then a nurse comes in with the breakfast tray, which she puts on a table beside JENNY, and then disappears)*

JENNY  Like some?

ANNA   No. *(Pause)* No, thank you.

JENNY   Can't you sit down?

ANNA   Yes.

JENNY   This is not going to be easy, Anna.

ANNA   Oh?

JENNY   For either you or me.

ANNA   Oh.

JENNY   I did something very stupid a few days ago.

ANNA   *(Looking at her)*   Did you?

JENNY   I tried to commit suicide.

ANNA   *(Looking at her)*   Did you?

JENNY   It's hard to explain how it could happen. You
might get the idea I didn't like you and Daddy, trying
to sneak off like that. But you must never think that.
*(Pause)* I'm more fond of you than of anyone else. You
and Grandma. And Daddy. *(Pause)* Have you never
just done something on the spur of the moment, without stopping to think?

ANNA   *(Looking at her)*   Yes. Perhaps.

*(The vulnerable open face, the lean straight shoulders, the soft
uncertain mouth, the beautiful broad hands with their dirty
blunt nails)*

JENNY   You must try to forgive me.

ANNA   I don't know what you mean.

*(The distance, the insurmountable distance.* JENNY *is mute and beaten)*

JENNY   Are you going back to camp today?

ANNA   There's a train in an hour.

JENNY   Do you have enough money?

ANNA   Yes thanks.

JENNY   Are you all having a nice time?

ANNA   Oh, not bad.

JENNY   Give my love to Lena and Karin.

ANNA   Yes.

JENNY   Is it on Friday that camp's over?

ANNA *(With a sigh)*   Yes.

JENNY   Couldn't we have dinner together, you and I, on your way through to Skåne? You get to town in the afternoon and your train doesn't leave until nine thirty in the evening. We could have dinner and then go to a movie. Wouldn't that be nice?

ANNA   Yes. Very nice.

JENNY   Well, you'd better go now, so that you don't miss the train.

(ANNA *gets up obediently.* JENNY *goes up to her, takes her face in both hands, and kisses her. The girl submits but looks embarrassed. Then she goes to the door, stops, turns around)*

JENNY *(Still hopeful)*   Yes?

(ANNA *gives her a long, hard look, and there is a glint of anguish in her gray eyes)*

ANNA   Will you do that again?

JENNY  No.

ANNA  How can I be sure?

JENNY  You must count on me to tell the truth.

ANNA  But do you know what you're saying?

JENNY  I think so.

ANNA  But you're not sure.

JENNY *(Vehemently)*  Just what are you getting at? Can't you understand *anything?*

ANNA  You've never liked me anyway.

(JENNY *stands with her arms hanging and looks at the girl over by the door, the fingers with the dirty bitten-down nails that won't stop fiddling with the little picture in a gold frame she wears around her neck. A long silence*)

ANNA  You haven't, you know. *(Pause)* Well, I must go now. *(Pause)* Don't worry. I'm good at managing on my own. Bye-bye.

(*And* ANNA *goes out, closing the door quietly behind her. A nurse looks in and asks if she can take the tray*)

JENNY  Yes, do. Thank you.


*That same afternoon* JENNY *returns to the house on the silent street.* GRANDMA *meets her in the hall. They embrace.*

GRANDMA   Are you better now?

JENNY   Much better.

GRANDMA   Why didn't you say something?

JENNY   There was nothing to say.

GRANDMA   I asked that Dr. Jacobi who called me up and he said you were under too much strain.

JENNY   Yes.

GRANDMA   And Erik rushing home like that.

JENNY   He's gone back, hasn't he?

GRANDMA   Oh yes. When he realized it wasn't so serious. That it was just strain.

JENNY   Did you have a talk?

GRANDMA   He was up for a little while, yes.

(*They are in* JENNY *'s room, and* GRANDMA *is helping her to unpack. The afternoon sun is very hot. The windows are wide open and the blinds are half down.* JENNY *sits on the bed.* GRANDMA *breaks off what she is doing*)

GRANDMA   You're tired. Shall I make the bed? Then you can lie down.

JENNY   No, thank you. There's no need.

GRANDMA   If you've been overdoing things you should go away for a few weeks and rest.

JENNY    It's impossible just now. Erneman won't be back for another two months. After that perhaps Erik and I will take a vacation. We had in fact planned a trip to Italy.

(JENNY *checks herself and looks at* GRANDMA. *It's as if she saw her for the first time. The old woman has sat down on a chair by the wall and the sunlight is shining in her face.* JENNY *discovers now that her grandmother is very old, that the clear blue-gray eyes are sad, that the firm mouth is not so firm, that she is not holding herself as straight as usual, that in some way* GRANDMA *has become smaller, not very much, but quite noticeably. And when she turns her face to* JENNY *and gives a little questioning smile, her head shakes almost imperceptibly but it shakes nevertheless, and the strong broad hands, the capable active hands, lie tired and idle in her lap*)

JENNY *(With sudden affection)*    What is it, Grandma?

GRANDMA    Grandpa wouldn't get up today. I nagged and scolded him but he just looked unhappy. It's probably a slight stroke, but you never know with Grandpa. The doctor has been—old Samuelson, you know. He just said for me to let Grandpa rest for a few days.

JENNY    And what do *you* think?

GRANDMA    I have a feeling in my bones that Grandpa will never get up again. He seems so terribly tired. (GRANDMA *can't say anything more for a while. She looks helplessly at* JENNY, *at her hands, out the window*) Well, that's the way it is. *(Pause)* I've been expecting this for several years. But it still feels funny when it comes. *(Pause)* Well, that's how it is.

(GRANDMA *gives a deep sigh and a tired little smile*)

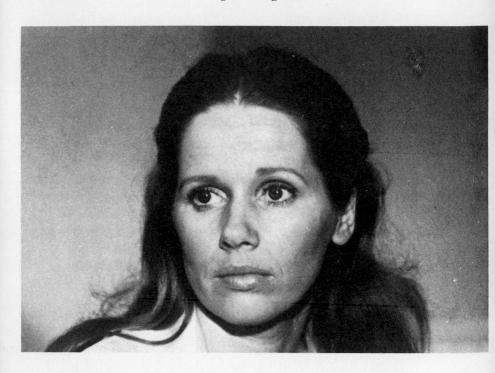

JENNY   I'll go in and say hello to him.

GRANDMA   Wouldn't you like something?

JENNY   No thanks. I had something to eat before leaving the hospital.

(GRANDMA *holds open the door.* GRANDPA *is lying in the big double bed, looking very small. As* GRANDMA *and* JENNY *approach he opens his eyes and looks at them anxiously*)

GRANDMA   Don't be nervous. I'll sit with you. I'm here all the time.

*(The anxious eyes grow calmer and he gives a little nod, then takes* GRANDMA *'s hand. She sits down beside the bed and pats him. Again and again she pats his hand.*

JENNY *stands for a long time at the door looking at the two old people and the way they belong together, moving slowly in toward the mysterious and awful point where they must part. She sees their humility and dignity and for a short moment she perceives—but forgets just as quickly—that love embraces all, even death)*

JENNY *(Softly)*  I think I'll go for a little walk.

GRANDMA  When you come back we'll have those chops that are in the refrigerator. There's some cold potato left too that you can fry. If the shop down at the corner is open, you might buy a lettuce.

*(*JENNY *nods and tiptoes out)*

*She has done her shopping at the store on the big tree-lined avenue. The traffic is busy, the offices have shut for the day, and there are a lot of people about. The sun shines brightly in the hot afternoon and the water glints in the canal. The huge treetops are rustling and the headlines of the evening papers are black and screaming.*

*She has stopped at a crosswalk with five or six others. She sees a tall woman, dressed in a white coat and white hat; her gray hair sticks out under the brim. She is holding a white cane and feeling her way with it against the curb. She is wearing sunglasses.*

JENNY  May I help you across the street perhaps?

(THE WOMAN *turns, and in a moment of surprise* JENNY *recognizes the passionate, pale face, the sarcastic smile. The dead, gouged-out eye*)

THE WOMAN   That's very kind of you, my dear. Thank you.

(JENNY *takes her by the arm and says, "Well, let's go then." They begin to walk slowly over the white markings of the crosswalk, while the other people hurry past without even glancing at them*)

## ABOUT THE AUTHOR

Ingmar Bergman has been one of Europe's leading film and theater directors for thirty years. The first of his films to be known in America was *The Seventh Seal*, which was followed by such great films as *Smiles of a Summer Night*, *Persona*, *The Virgin Spring*, *Through a Glass Darkly*, *Cries and Whispers*, and *Scenes from a Marriage*.

Bergman has received every major American and European film prize and is considered by many to be the world's greatest living film director.